FOR REFERENCE

CHILDREN OF POVERTY

STUDIES ON THE EFFECTS
OF SINGLE PARENTHOOD,
THE FEMINIZATION OF POVERTY,
AND HOMELESSNESS

edited by
STUART BRUCHEY
ALLAN NEVINS PROFESSOR EMERITUS
COLUMBIA UNIVERSITY

A GARLAND SERIES

AFRICAN-AMERICAN AND WHITE ADOLESCENT MOTHERS

Can Early Intervention Programs Help?

FAITH L. SAMPLES

GARLAND PUBLISHING, INC.
A MEMBER OF THE TAYLOR & FRANCIS GROUP
NEW YORK & LONDON / 1998

Copyright © 1998 Faith L. Samples
All rights reserved

Library of Congress Cataloging-in-Publication Data

Samples, Faith L., 1964–
  African-American and white adolescent mothers : can early intervention programs help? / Faith L. Samples.
       p.   cm. — (Children of poverty)
  Includes bibliographical references and index.
  ISBN 0-8153-3158-4 (alk. paper)
  1. Afro-American teenage mothers—Social conditions.
  2. White teenage mothers—United States—Social conditions.
  3. Children of teenage mothers—United States—Social conditions.
  4. Afro-American teenage mothers—Services for. 5. White teenage mothers—Services for—United States. 6. Children of teenage mothers—Services for—United States. 7. Visiting nurses—United States.   I. Title. II. Series.
  E185.86.S247 1998
  306.874'3—dc21
                                                           98-15136

Printed on acid-free, 250-year-life paper
Manufactured in the United States of America

To my husband, Leon, for always cheering in my corner and to our daughter, Kariamu, for defining life's real challenges and for keeping me grounded in reality.

Contents

Tables	ix
Preface	xi-xii
Acknowledgments	xiii
Chapter One: Statement of the Problem	3
Overview	3-8
Rationale for Study	8-9
Purpose and Objectives	10
Format of the Study	11
Chapter Two: Literature Review	13
Social Support	14-18
Social Network Influences on Adolescent Pregnancy and Childbearing	19-20
Social Context of Teenage Pregnancy	20-24
Availability and Utilization of Support	25-29
Racial Differences in Adolescent Social Support	29-32
Early Intervention	32-33
Problems of Methodology	33-34
Effectiveness of Early Intervention Programs	35-43
Early Intervention for Adolescent Mothers	43-48
Summary	49
Chapter Three: Methodology	51
Present Study	52-53
Sample and Procedure	53-54

Combining Treatment Groups and Social Support Operationalized	54-56
Methods of Analysis	56
Limitations of the Data	57-58
Chapter Four: Results	59
Overview	59
Anticipated Child Care and Chore Support	60-61
Anticipated Versus Actual Labor/Delivery Support	62-63
Source of Anticipated Support at Intake	64-66
Comparison of Interest in Pregnancy with Interest Shown in Child	67-70
Reaction to Child at Birth and Subsequent Social Support	71-76
Summary	76-77
Chapter Five: Discussion	81
Overview	81-82
Impact of Treatment Condition on Social Support	82-85
The Moderating Effect of Race on Social Support and Anticipated Support for Labor/Delivery, Child Care, and Chores	86-90
Support Person Behavior and Child Care and Chore Support	90-92
Explanation of Lack of Effects of the PEIP	92-93
Chapter Six: Implications for Policy and Conclusion	95-98
Bibliography	99-108
Index	109-111

Tables

Table 3.1	Support Variables	57
Table 4.1	Anticipated Child Care and Chore Support, by Treatment Group and Race	61
Table 4.2	Perceived versus Actual Support during Labor and Delivery, by Treatment Group	62
Table 4.3	Perceived versus Actual Support during Labor and Delivery, by Race	64
Table 4.4	Source of Support at Intake, by Treatment Group	65
Table 4.5	Source of Support at Intake, by Race	67
Table 4.6	Husband/Boyfriend Interest in Pregnancy as a Predictor of Interest in the Child, by Treatment Group	69
Table 4.7	Husband/Boyfriend Interest in Pregnancy as a Predictor of Interest in the Child, by Race	71
Table 4.8	Reaction to and Level of Interaction with Infant as Compared with Child Care and Chore Support Over Time, by Treatment Group	74
Table 4.9a	Reaction to and Level of Interaction with Infant, by Race	75
Table 49b	Child Care and Chore Support Over Time, by Race	78
Table 4.10	Chronological Summary of Significant Main Effects, by Treatment Group and Race	79

Preface

When I was growing up, it seemed I was one of only a small few adolescent girls in my predominantly African American neighborhood or amongst my largely White peers (with whom I went to private school outside my community) who was not sexually active. While this activity was not as likely to result in pregnancy among my White peers, they were as sexually active as the African American girls in my neighborhood. I wondered sometimes, if not more so, since it seemed all they talked about at school was who they had been with.

My curiosity about the matter of adolescent sexuality had been sparked years before and was only being further fueled by what seemed to be a continuation of what I had already deemed to be a "teenage baby revolution." The occurrence of adolescent pregnancy was pervasive in my community and had caught my attention several years before I officially joined the ranks of adolescence. Upon reaching adolescence, I noted the trends in adolescent pregnancy and out-of-wedlock births had abated in the least, and, in fact, seemed to be growing in rapid numbers.

I had often wondered how young girls managed their own needs as teenagers with the insistent demands of infants and children. What factors determined their success or failure? Do those same factors apply for White adolescent mothers that seemed relevant for African American adolescent mothers? How important is social to adolescents generally? In my community, and many others like it, support was a given that was often supplied in sufficient abundance. But, I wondered if the same were true of White adolescents.

It has long since been my belief that the factors that motivated African American adolescents to have children were distinctly different from those of their sexually active White peers. With this in mind, it seemed logical that previous efforts to alleviate the problem of "babies having babies" were less than effective. The tendency has been to address the problem globally, applying universal programs with little consideration for the diversity of the populations being served. This study sought to examine the influence of an early intervention program on the social support networks of African American and White adolescent mothers and to theory of universal applicability to the test. A mirage of prevention efforts have attempted to address the problems of teenage pregnancy and out-of-wedlockbirths, yet our understanding of the motivating factors for and the solution to the problem(s) have remained elusive.

If the goal is to truly ameliorate the problem of adolescent pregnancy, our primary objective must be to understand the needs, cultural backgrounds, and parenting practices of respective groups within our diverse society. Until such time as we, as researcher, practitioners, and policy makers, devote our energies to understanding the differential needs of communities and families, we will continue to fall short of the mark for instituting programs and policies for effective change.

Acknowledgments

I would like to give thanks to God, first and foremost, fore all things are possible through Him. Considerable thanks also goes to John Eckenrode, Don Barr, Theodore Lowi, and Alan Hahn for their assistance in helping me frame this work and for challenging me to write from the heart on the toughest issues.

The patience and encouragement of my husband, Leon, during points of frustration is most sincerely appreciated. Finally, a very big thank you goes out to all of the people who have always believed in my talent and ability.

African-American and White
Adolescent Mothers

CHAPTER 1
Statement of the Problem

The plight of America's children and families has come to the forefront of discussions by health, education, and social service professionals, as well as by the nation's policy-makers. Contemporary families are confronted with stressors stemming from an array of current social conditions, including structural changes in the family, economic problems due to under- or unemployment single and teenage parenthood, and the increased incidence of child maltreatment. Adolescent and out-of-wedlock births stand among these as especially challenging problems. They represent a socio-cultural phenomenon commonly associated with social, economic, and medical problems for both mother and child.

For instance, it is well known that infants born to adolescents have higher rates of mortality than those of older women. This is coupled with the fact that a disproportionate number of adolescent pregnancies take place outside the confines of marriage (estimates range from 65% to 80%). When examining these trends across racial lines, the complexity of the issue grows markedly. African American teenagers arguably have the highest fertility rate of any teenage population in the world (Davis, 1988), a problem compounded by an out-of-wedlock pregnancy rate estimated at 91.2% (Rosenbaum, Layton, & Liu, 1991). During a time of general decline in the nation's infant mortality rate, the rate at which African American infants were dying during their first year of life remained equal to about twice that of Whites. And, although rates of non-marital pregnancy for African American youth remained relatively stable while those of Whites increased steadily in recent decades, the rate of birth among African American teenagers is still nearly double that of White adolescents.

Increases in the birth rates among young, unmarried women have reportedly resulted in a disproportionate number of children conceived and reared in familial, societal, and economic conditions that are less than optimal for healthy growth and development (Brooks-Gunn & Chase-Lansdale, 1991; Coates & Van Widenfelt, 1991; Furstenberg, 1976; Prenatal/Early Infancy Project [PEIP] Final Report, 1983). Evidence of the long-term consequences of early and out-of-wedlock parenting show fairly consistent and enduring disadvantages for both mother and child. Negative socioeconomic outcomes are predicted to result from the decreased likelihood that women will complete high school or find adequate and stable employment. There are reports that suggest that poor and young women are more likely to experience medical complications due to late or inadequate prenatal care. Additionally, data have shown that the ways in which young mothers interact with their children may increase infants' risks of developmental delay.

Studies of health outcomes among teenagers who carry their pregnancies to term have found evidence to refute the notion that adolescent childbearing is detrimental to the health and well-being of women and children. When early and adequate prenatal care are provided, the risks of maternal and infant mortality, prematurity, and low birth weight babies are reduced considerably. Concern persists, however, about the ability of young mothers to engage in optimal parenting practices. The question is often one of how well young mothers can meet the needs of their children and understand or resolve the tasks of parenthood when they themselves are grappling with issues inherent in adolescence as a unique stage of development.

The social context in which pregnancy takes place and the availability of social support have been shown to have important implications for the adaptation to and performance in the parenting role. Several researchers (e.g., Colletta, 1981; Crockenberg, 1987; Furstenberg, 1976) have found social from significant others to positively impact upon the parenting practices of young mothers, and ultimately, on the developmental outcomes of children. Supportive social relationships promote satisfaction with the mothering role, which, in turn, is related to increased feelings of self-worth, an internal locus of control, decreased stress reactions, and a reduction in depression and anxiety. To the extent that such relationships influence parental attitudes and behaviors specifically, the impact on child

Statement of the Problem

developmental outcomes would seem to be strengthened through improvements in the overall quality of parenting.

Social support is a concept frequently used to refer to the ways in which human relationships are structured to provide help and assistance during times of need. It involves the sharing of tasks, feelings, and responsibilities, as well as the exchange of information, resources (personal, material, and financial), and affection. Essentially, social support is the sharing and exchanging of the everyday experiences of human life that take place within families and among friends, relatives, co-workers, neighbors, and acquaintances. The informality, mutuality, and reciprocity characteristic of social support has historically made it a positive structural force in the lives of many people.

Literature on social support offers strong theoretical and empirical evidence that attests to the proposition that social support buffers the effects of stress and promotes health (Gottlieb, 1988; Pearlin, 1985). The nature and significance of social support varies so that the type or source of support needed to facilitate psychological well-being may differ depending on the type of adjustment to be made. In addition to variations in the type and source of social required by different people, there are also differences in the nature of supportive relationships across racial or ethnic groups. African American families much more than white families tend to exist in an extended helping network. The role of significant others in the lives of African Americans has been the subject of both theoretical formulation and empirical research. Essentially, African American families exist within a family context that extends far beyond formal kinship ties to include non-family members who take on kinship roles. Being embedded in an extended network of family, friends, and other community members is very much a part of their cultural heritage and is often attributed to the number of stressors confronting this population on an almost daily basis. The sense of community comes from the fact that the larger group is relatively equal in its need for support. Consequently, help and support are extended throughout the community, first through kinship ties and then through sources that take on kinship qualities. Variations notwithstanding, reports have consistently shown that people who have supportive interpersonal relationships tend to fare better when confronted with stressful life events than those without such supports.

The convergence of this scientific evidence with the reality that the United States leads nearly all other industrialized nations in adolescent fertility has been an impetus for action among policy-makers and practitioners. Compelled by the need to educate, nurture, and provide positive reinforcement to child rearing families, government and agency decision-makers have assigned priority to the development and implementation of support interventions. To the extent that these interventions arise from and affect the natural social contexts in which people live, they are attractive to practitioners and the public at large.

Social support has its origins in the contexts of communities, where neighbors, extended family, friends, and others have assisted families by providing support in a variety of forms. Data show that social support is a resource much more accessible, culturally valid, and acceptable than services offered by traditional mental health and social service agencies. In light of this evidence, interventions that make the mobilization of informal resources their focal point not only enhance their cost efficiency but also increase the likelihood that they will reach historically under-served populations and effect changes conducive to health, well-being, and adjustment to major life events or transitions.

Use of the social support construct as a component of early interventions suggests the emergence of a paradigm that brings together the field of social science with human service delivery agencies (Powell, 1980). Presumably, efforts to improve the interpersonal support networks of families while making provisions for the delivery of more formal services provides an optimal primary prevention strategy for addressing the needs of disadvantaged families. However, interventions employing the social support concept have yielded mixed results. Differences in reported findings have been attributed, in part, to differences in methodological design, variations in the definition of family support, and a lack of congruence between the way in which social support is used within the context of interventions and the way it is measured as a factor affecting the outcomes of some interventions.

To date, evidence about the role of social support on maternal and child health and development within the framework of social interventions has been unclear. Relatively few studies have evaluated the role social support plays in interventions to determine whether it mediates program effectiveness. Similarly, there is a paucity of intervention studies that investigate the moderating effect of social support on outcome variables. The need to explore the nature and function of social support and its relationship to the child rearing practices of socially and economically disadvantaged families, both

Statement of the Problem

independently and within the framework of interventions, is great. It is only through such efforts that researchers, policy-makers, and service delivery professionals will truly be able to determine the types of programs that best serve the needs of at-risk children and their families.

Early studies of the impact of social interventions revealed that the most effective means by which to affect child outcomes was to address the needs, problems, and concerns of families. The move has been toward interventions that address the health and developmental needs of at-risk children via improving the life circumstances of their parents. There is mounting evidence to suggest that intervention programs targeted at affecting the natural support systems of parents may have an immediate and long-term impact on the lives of children by improving maternal functioning (Achenbach, Phares, & Howell, 1990; Lally, Mangione, & Honig, 1988; Madden, O'Hara, & Levenstein, 1984; Seitz, Rosenbaum, & Apfel, 1985; Siegel, Bauman, Schaefer, Saunders, & Ingram, 1980).

Although a number of approaches have been used to achieve these goals, home visitation appears to have received the most widespread public and policy attention. Home visitation has a long and rich history that spans more than a century in the United States. It had been an integral part of this country's public health strategy for addressing the needs of at-risk children and their families before falling from favor and becoming restricted in its focus (Olds, 1983). In more recent years, it has gained a new appeal, as it has been shown to prevent death and injury while also promoting the health and development of disadvantaged children.

As a result, legislative proposals have been put forth requesting an increase in the current level of federal support for home visitation services. For example, in 1989, the National Commission to Prevent Infant Mortality advocated programs of home visiting for at-risk families with young children. A recommendation from the Office of Technology Assessment suggested that such services be included as policy options for counteracting health, educational, and developmental problems among our nation's children. Growing interest in alleviating problems confronting young and single mothers rearing children is continually guiding policy initiatives toward home-based interventions that make the identification and treatment of such problems considerably easier.

The best evidence for the effectiveness of home visitation as a means of improving maternal and child outcomes is derived from a study conducted in a semi-rural community in Upstate New York using professionally trained nurses—the Prenatal/Early Infancy Program (PEIP). The PEIP investigated the effect of nurse home visitation services on pregnancy outcomes and early child rearing in socially disadvantaged families. Using an ecological framework, wherein parental behavior was viewed as the most forceful and potentially alterable influence on fetal and infant development, the study employed randomized trials of a predominantly White sample of 400 families. In addition to assessing the effectiveness of the intervention given the risk characteristics of the sample (i.e., poor, single, and young), the study also sought to determine the process through which program effectiveness was achieved. Furthermore, it provided a cost-benefit analysis which estimated federal government savings for an investment in home visitation services. Findings from the Elmira study have been instrumental in renewing the interest in home visitation services at both the state and the national level.

RATIONALE FOR STUDY

Emerging theories of the ecology of human development have spurred a number of studies examining the role and effectiveness of social support in buffering the effects of stressful life events and in promoting health and well-being. Without question, increasing attention has been given to the role of naturally forming support systems as targets of prevention efforts on behalf of America's at-risk families. The specific reasons why support interventions have attracted the attention of health and human service practitioners and the nation's policy-makers differ slightly. Nonetheless, there seem to be three common reasons for their general attractiveness as measures by which to improve the life circumstances of women with children.

First, the scientific literature on the protective and health-promoting features of supportive social relationships is quite voluminous. Moreover, the fact that the provision for support occurs through exchanges among lay people to their mutual benefit necessarily reduces costs where interventions focus on the mobilization of informal resources. Finally, given the structural properties of social support, it seems highly likely that previously unserved and underserved populations will be reached if emphasis is placed on enhancing the natural support systems in which they exist. Historical evidence seems to point to people's preference for engaging in the

Statement of the Problem

exchange of mutual aid rather than seeking assistance from institutionally-based professionals.

The move toward support interventionssuggests the emergence of a paradigm that brings social sciences and human services agencies together. Rather than approach the problems confronting disadvantaged children in a manner that fails to produce change at the family level, support interventions enable service provision that is family-centered. In this way, the benefits of supportive social relationships translate into direct and indirect effects on children through improvements in the family's overall quality of life. Studies of support interventions, to date, have not yielded entirely positive results due to rather narrow definitions of the support construct (Olds & Kitzman, 1990). While social intervention programs provide services labeled "social support," relatively few studies have examined the independent or mediating effect of this construct.

According to Weiss (1988), the availability and use of formal support systems and the reliance on informal support networks are considered an essential part of intervention programs, yet few researchers have tested the consequences of such support for parental or family functioning, parent-child interaction, or personal well-being. It is when social support is measured as a mediating or possible outcome variable that the true impact of social interventions are assessed, thereby providing opportunities which enable researchers and program developers to look past the correlational relationships of social support. In so doing, it opens up the possibility of exploring causal relationships within the context of early intervention.

Intervention studies such as the PEIP which have emphasized that social support along with education, may result in positive effects on children's developmental status through improvements in the care giving quality of parents. The evidence seems to be consistent with other findings that suggest a positive relationship between supportive social ties and maternal adjustment to the parenting role, satisfaction with parenting, and more positive attitudes and behaviors. The lack of data on the role of social support within the context of early intervention programs and the promise provided by the Elmira data serve as the basis for conducting the present study.

PURPOSE AND OBJECTIVES

The primary purpose of the study was to investigate the effect of the PEIP on social support among poor, unmarried adolescent mothers. In addition, the study sought to assess change in social support over time. The study also examined the extent to which the PEIP impacted social support as function of race to determine how the support networks of African American and White women differed, if at all.

The study addressed the problems of adolescent pregnancy and single parenthood, as well as assessed the impact of this particular early intervention program on the health and well-being of African American children and their families. The specific objectives of the study are listed below:

1. Determine differences in the impact of the intervention on and in the support networks of African American and White adolescent mothers.
2. Determine whether social support is enhanced over time as a function of nurse home visits.

Literature on the consequences of early childbearing for both mother and child make the assessment of early intervention programs necessary as a means of determining their ability to enhance the natural support systems of young mothers with children. The purpose of this study was to investigate the impact of the PEIP on social support for adolescent mothers, with a special interest in the differential role of social support for African American and White adolescent mothers.

This study does not address the bigger question of whether social support improves the child rearing behaviors of adolescent mothers. Instead, it examines the differential impact of a comprehensive early intervention program on the social support networks of African American and White adolescents. In so doing, it helps to further inform practitioners, researchers, and policy-makers alike about the role social support plays in adolescents' adjustment to motherhood. This is particularly important when referring to social support within the context of early interventions designed to ameliorate or prevent adolescent pregnancy. New information about intervention strategies that work best for different groups of people aid in the development and implementation of more effective programs.

Statement of the Problem

FORMAT OF BOOK

In chapter 2, I will review the literature on both social support and early intervention programs to assess their effects on the health and development of socially and environmentally disadvantaged families. In so doing, I will discuss the conceptual and methodological problems that have plagued these areas of research and highlight specific factors that result in differences in reported findings. An examination of racial and ethnic group differences will also be included in this chapter.

Chapter 3 provides background information on the PEIP Study—the larger study from which the data for this work were drawn. Following that, I will discuss the design, sampling procedure, and limitations of the present study. In Chapter 4, the findings of my analyses are reported. In Chapter 5, I offer explanations for reported findings, followed by a discussion of the implications for policy in Chapter 6.

CHAPTER 2
Literature Review

Adolescents and their infants are at risk for social, medical, and economic problems that require comprehensive health care programs integrating medical, educational, and psychological components. Although the past 20 years have witnessed the development of a number of interventions designed to prevent or ameliorate the negative consequences of premature childbearing, there are relatively few experimentally-designed, longitudinal studies of the efficacy of such programs. Of these, only a small number have samples of adolescent mothers. Consequently, very little is known about teenage mothers who participate in these programs.

In addition to these shortcomings in the intervention literature, there is also a lack of clarity regarding the role of social support in promoting health among mothers and their infants. The social support concept has become an important feature of social interventions, yet the support element of many early intervention studies focusing on reproductive health has been virtually absent. Evidence suggesting that socially supported mothers benefit from improved health outcomes; adjust better to the mothering role; and exhibit more effective parenting attitudes and behaviors would seemingly provide a sound basis for inclusion of social support as a program component of such studies.

Certainly, evidence for the relationship between social support and health in general raises the question of whether social support is good for the health of mothers and infants. But, because the social support literature did not really begin to take form until the late 1970's, any discussion about social support and pregnancy outcomes begs an entire series of other important and, perhaps, more difficult questions. Some of these include the following: What is social support? Does social facilitate the adjustment to motherhood among adolescents? What is the relationship between social and the parenting practices of adolescent mothers? Does social support vary as a function of race? Finally, can social support be enhanced through early intervention? This study focuses on the relevance of social support to parenting practices among adolescent mothers. However, in order to do this in a meaningful way, it is necessary to first place the issues in the broader context of research on social support.

SOCIAL SUPPORT

The health-promoting potential of social support has attracted the attention of researchers from a host of social science and health-related fields. The significance of supportive social relationships formed between individuals and others with whom they interact, including relatives, friends, neighbors, partners, co-workers, and other acquaintances, has been recognized as an important factor that helps to explain adjustment to major life events. The interaction between individuals and important others constitutes networks that are viewed as relational structures through which support is requested, coping skills are reinforced, and nuturance is provided (Garbarino, 1983). The social support network is a structure which provides regular patterns of support through a range of interpersonal exchanges that provide individuals with information, advice, emotional reassurance, and instrumental or financial assistance (Pilisuk & Parks, 1980). Conceptually, social support has gained in popularity as a positive structural force in the lives of many people due to its informality, mutuality, and reciprocity.

Data suggest that the utilization of various network members differs depending on the needs of the individual (Powell, 1980). The type of support requested is generally in keeping with the type of adjustment required. While there is certainly some variation in the source and type of support on which individuals rely, the provision of support appears to come in one of three predominant forms: 1) emotional support, which is demonstrated through the expression of care, concern, and acceptance as a member of a mutually obligated group; 2) instrumental or material support, which refers largely to problems whose resolutions require financial resources (aid is provided both directly and indirectly and take various forms, ranging from gifts, to loans, to child care); and 3) informational or intangible support, which provides access to more formal services via advice, information, or referrals.

Attempts to understand the role of social support in the promotion and maintenance of health and well-being has resulted in efforts to determine how it impacts upon the lives of individuals. Does social support have a direct effect on the adjustment to major life stress, or does it act as a buffer against the negative effects of stressful life events? Barrera (1981) suggests that the response to these questions vary among researchers since either effect may be linked to the diverse conceptions and measures of social support. Presently, there is no unified (Cohen & Syme, 1985). The lack of clarity in both the definition of social support and in the conceptualization of the meaning of social support, its role in health and behavior, or even how it is measured has hampered research in this area.

The problem of how to best define social support dates back several decades, as was illustrated in an examination of early interpretations of the construct. In reviewing the work of John Cassel, Sidney Cobb, and Gerald Caplan, Gottlieb (1983) unveiled problems in definition that involved differences in the scope, type, and structure of social support. According to Gottlieb, Cassel's definition of social support involved feedback conveyed in signs and signals from primary group members that correct deviations from course at the behavioral, cognitive, and emotional levels. Because of the broad scope of this definition, it would be difficult to determine how to optimize feedback. Cobb's definition, while more detailed, fails to account for forms of support that involve the rendering of tangible goods or services. According to Cobb, the primary function of supports is to provide information which leads to the belief that one is cared for and loved, valued and esteemed, and a member of a mutual obligatory network. Unlike Cassel and Cobb, Caplan uses the term "system" to refer to the support provided by significant others. He defines support systems as continuing social aggregates that provide opportunities for feedback about self and validation about others. The problem with this definition is that it does not elaborate on the structural properties of support systems, nor does it deal with the process by which they are formed.

More recent problems concerning issues of definition involve distinguishing between social support and social networks. House and Kahn (1985) see both concepts as related to a number of different aspects of social relationships. They suggest that social support is sometimes conceptually defined in terms of the existence or quantity of social relationships, the structure that such relationships take, and the functional content of supportive social relationships. It is their belief that, in contrast, social networks refer most often to the structure of an individual's relationships with supportive contacts. Consequently, they argue, social networks must be considered part of the general domain of social support. Contrary to this conceptualization of social support, Cochran, Larner, Riley, Gunnarsson, and Henderson (1990) suggest that most researchers employing the concept of social support rely on the work of Cobb, where the primary focus is on the psychological state of the recipient. Social network is distinguished from the concept of social support by its broader focus on specific linkages among a defined set of persons. According to these researchers, the emphasis is not only on the characteristics of the network structure but also on the various types of exchanges that take place between group members (i.e., structure and content). Such differences in the way in which social support is defined, both conceptually and operationally, helps to explain the existing controversy surrounding definitional issues.

Likewise, the lack of agreement among researchers on which measure to use in operationalizing the social support construct has presented problems. Gottlieb contends (1981; 1983) that this lack of agreement has made it difficult to draw firm conclusions about its actual effects on the life stress process or to compare and summarize studies that investigate its empirical effects on health. According to Gottlieb, current measures of social support take three dominant forms, each with a different level of analysis—i.e., the macro, mezzo, and micro levels.

At the macroscopic level, the focal point of research is the relationship between the existence or quantity of an individual's social contacts and his well-being. The underlying idea is that the lack of social support results in social isolation. Measures of the number of social ties one possesses, while very crude assessments of the nature of social support have been described as relatively objective, reliable, and unconfounded with measures of other relevant variables such as stress and health (House and Kahn, 1985). The mezzo level uses the social network approach to study the ways in which social relationships are linked to an individual's health and well-being. Here the focus is on structural differences within a range of social relationships and on the way these differential patterns affect access to resources required for adjustment to stressful life events. This approach boasts a number of advantages; nevertheless, there are issues concerning its usefulness in determining the association between aspects of social relationships and health, as well as with the cost effectiveness of collecting and processing the amount of data necessary to fully characterize the structure of social networks.

Studies measuring social support in terms of its structure and supportive content comprise those at the micro level of analysis. This approach, according to Gottlieb (1983), emphasizes the quality of social relationships and seeks to determine the adequacy of the psychosocial exchange in these relationships. However, in a review of existing measures of social support, House and Kahn (1985) found that when measuring the functional content of lines of quantity or availability versus quality or adequacy, but distinctions were also made with respect to the source (e.g., family, friend, partner) and type of support (e.g., instrumental). Moreover, measures differed in whether they sought information about the perceived availability of support or about the occurrence of actual supportive behaviors. While few negative results have been found when measuring support in this manner, the wide array of measures used and the generally weak research designs employed have made delineation of a single, universal measure almost impossible (House & Kahn, 1985).

The measurement issue in the study of social support is further complicated by the almost sole reliance on self-reports of the support mobilization process. Support mobilization involves the ability of individuals to solicit organized assistance from members of their support network in times of identified need. Research on all aspects of support has relied most heavily upon subjects' reports of the number of persons who came to their aid, what resources supports provided, and how the support was perceived. Both Gottlieb (1981) and House and Kahn (1985) state that measurement of the social support construct is still in the developmental stages. They contend that until more progress is made toward reconciling contrasting measures and toward developing valid and reliable instruments, the extent to which social support contributes to the prediction of health outcomes will be difficult to determine with any degree of confidence.

Literature on the health-promoting effects of social support also suggests deficiencies in several other respects. Pearlin (1985), for example, suggests that studies conducted in this area fail to address questions of how and under what conditions support buffers the effects of stress. According to Gottlieb and Wagner (1991), researchers have not thoroughly investigated the personal, situational, and relationship contingencies that affect the receipt and provision of support. Furthermore, there is little knowledge about the process involved in the mobilization of social support. Eckenrode (1983), Eckenrode and Gore (1981), and Eckenrode and Wethington (1990) highlight the importance of marshaling social support in the presence of stress and the need for researchers to make clear distinctions between perceived and actual support.

Evidence clearly suggests the need for more specificity around definitional, conceptual, and measurement issues. This is particularly true when the focus of social support is shifted from resources that may be gained to the stress-inducing transactions indicative of some social interactions. It has been suggested that the influence of social network members may extend far beyond that of "supportive" social ties to involve both costs and benefits (Cochran et al., 1990). To suggest that social support holds a universal and intrinsic benefit would be misleading since there is evidence to counter such a notion. For instance, social support has been associated with psychological distress (Barrera, 1981; Lindblad-Goldberg et al., 1980).

Gottlieb (1983) warns researchers against romantic views of social support wherein the support system is perceived as unconditionally helpful and always empathetic. Likewise, Riley and Eckenrode (1990) suggest that the existence of social ties does not ensure translation into social support. These researchers highlight the need for measures that examine the true balance of influences that stem from social relations—the potentially detrimental as well as the sustaining or positive influences.

Deficiencies in the conceptualization and measurement notwithstanding, the buffering effects of social support are well documented (Turner, Grindstaff, & Phillips, 1990; Cooley & Unger, 1991; Richardson, Barbour, & Bubenzer, 1991). Even when burdensome or stressful exchanges are taken into account, the preponderance of studies in this area emphasize the significance of support received from kin, neighbors, friends, or other lay persons. The evidence points to a strong and positive correlation between the availability of social support and the adaptation to life stress.

Literature Review

SOCIAL NETWORK INFLUENCES ON ADOLESCENT PREGNANCY AND CHILDBEARING

Life change has been identified as playing a primary role in the generation of stress (Furstenberg and Crawford, 1978), particularly when life event changes necessitate a redefinition of roles (Wandersman, Wandersman, & Kahn, 1980). Several researchers argue that adolescent pregnancy and parenthood represent a crisis period that usually results in psychological stress for both adolescents and their families (Field, Widmayer, Stringer, & Ignatoff, 1980; McHenry, Walters, & Johnson, 1979; Phipps-Yonas, 1980). In addition to the social, economic, and child rearing problems experienced by young mothers, they are believed to experience an additional source of stress as a consequence of their psychological immaturity. DeLissovoy (1973) suggests that adolescents are not adequately prepared to cope with the pressures that result from the accelerated role transition to adult responsibilities.

As previously stated, much of the early research on adolescent pregnancy focused on the health outcomes for both mother and child. Later studies highlighted the negative short- and long-term social and economic disadvantages the children of such mothers would necessarily endure. More recent studies have begun to contradict many of the widely held beliefs associated with early parenthood. Early pregnancy and parenting have not been found to be inherently detrimental to the survival of infants. It is the contention of several researchers (Barnett, 1991; Brooks-Gunn & Chase-Lansdale, 1991; Geronimus, 1987) that few, if any, differences exist between the children of adolescent and older mothers when early and adequate prenatal care are provided. The likelihood that medical complications will arise, they argue, is linked not as much to age as it is to poverty. And, contrary to popular belief, early childbearing does not invariably result in educational failure or adverse social and economic hardships. Upchurch and McCarthy (1990) found that while adolescent pregnancy does indeed place both mother and child at a socioeconomic disadvantage, they fare no worse than women in similar circumstances who have postponed childbearing.

Despite these more encouraging reports, there remains considerable concern regarding adolescents' adjustment to the parenting role and the quality of care they are able to provide for their children. Barrera (1981), while perceiving pregnancy and childbirth as particularly disruptive, contends that they are events whose impact on psychological well-being may feasibly be influenced by the presence or absence of social support. There is also data which indicate that the social context in which pregnancy takes place and the availability of social support have important implications for positive parenting practices among young mothers. Studies examining the social contexts surrounding young mothers and their infants have attempted to understand the circumstances which lend themselves to the successful management of the responsibilities of parenthood at such an early age.

SOCIAL CONTEXT OF TEENAGE PREGNANCY

The social context of adolescent pregnancy and childbearing may buffer the negative effects of early parenthood on children's development in a number of ways. In particular, living within an extended family system has been shown to positively impact adolescents' adjustment to parenthood. For example, Zuckerman et al. (1979) conducted a study of inner city adolescents to test the ability of young mothers to simultaneously cope with the demands of adolescence and parenthood. Their findings did not support their hypothesis that adolescent mothers and their infants were at considerable risk for adjustment and developmental problems. Rather, these investigators found adolescents to adapt to their role as mothers quite well in the presence of a supportive social network. Although only 8% of these young mothers were married, 95% lived with extended family and 81% reported having the support of the child's father.

Much like the women in the previous study, a number of adolescent mothers in Furstenberg and Crawford's (1978) study not only lived with their parents, they both perceived and used them as supports. Family support aided in the adjustment to parenting by enabling teenage mothers to complete the tasks of adolescence while serving in the adult role of mother. More specifically, teens who lived at home following the birth of their child were more likely to return to and graduate from school, to secure stable employment, and to avoid repeat pregnancies. Mothers who moved out after their deliveries tended not to return to and graduate from high school, to be unemployed, and to be receiving public assistance at the five year follow-up.

Literature on the support networks of adolescent mothers suggests that differences in support can enhance the personal and social adjustment of young mothers. Wasserman, Brunelli, & Rauh (1990b) found the living arrangements of adolescent and adult mothers to differentially affect the amount, type, and source of support received. Significant differences were found in the amount and type of support received between the two groups, with adolescents receiving the higher levels of all forms of social support. Both receipt of and sources from which support was obtained were related to living arrangements. Adolescents relied more heavily on their own mothers, whereas adults were more likely to receive support from friends. The authors report that, irrespective of age, mothers residing with their own mothers had significantly more tangible support (i.e., child care and financial assistance) and more guidance (i.e., health information and child care advice) than women living under any other circumstances.

Colletta and Lee (1983) suggest that adolescent mothers have better mental health and less stress when they are able to achieve the tasks of adolescence and motherhood simultaneously. This was certainly true of adolescents in their study, in which a sample of African American adolescents was investigated. Adolescents who remained in school after the birth of their child as compared to those who dropped out, received the most support. The authors report that support was highest for those with the greatest need for child care, those who returned to school, and those who worked.

Support for the notion that the life circumstances of adolescent mothers affect the level of social support they receive was provided by Schilmoeller, Baranowski, and Higgins (1991), who found adolescent mothers to be receiving significantly more formal support services than their older counterparts. Although there were reportedly no significant group differences in mothers' interactions with their support networks, general life and parenting satisfaction were strongly associated with the quality of social interactions and perceived family support among adolescent mothers. The higher the quality of reported interactions and the greater the adolescents' perceived family support, the more satisfied they were at 12 months postpartum. The same did not hold true for older mothers. In contrast to this finding were results of Klein and Cordell's (1987) study. As was anticipated, adolescents living with extended family reported larger support networks. Unfortunately, network size turned out to be related to increased anxiety and resentment about the parenting role. Marriage, on the other hand, was highly correlated with life satisfaction.

Differences in the level of support is even more keenly demonstrated in studies by Unger and Wandersman (1985; 1988). In two longitudinal studies younger and older adolescent were examined to assess the influence of social support on their adjustment. A strong relationship was reported between family support and adolescents' feelings of adjustment in both samples. However, reports of life satisfaction indicated greater levels of perceived support among younger mothers. Increased life satisfaction was found for older adolescent mothers at 1 month postpartum, while the life satisfaction of younger mothers was related to perceived support both before and after the child's birth. These findings are in keeping with the notion that adolescent parents may be at greater risk of experiencing stress in the parenting role and are, therefore, most in need of social support.

This would seem to apply within the adolescent population itself, with younger adolescents requiring and receiving more support than their slightly older adolescent counterparts (Barth, Schinke, & Maxwell, 1983). According to findings by Mayfield-Brown (1989) this is, in fact, true. In her study of adolescent mothers, the author found that younger mothers continued to live with and depend on their parents for support. The support received enabled these mothers to continue aspects of adolescence such as school completion. Mayfield-Brown contends that the dependence on family support is due largely to limited options confronted by mothers who have relatively little formal education and who are too young to compete effectively in the labor force.

Wasserman, Rauh, Brunelli, Garcia-Castro, and Necos (1990a) argue that the higher level of support common to adolescent mothers serves as a buffer against the negative effects of early parenting. Evidence for the buffering effect for perceived intimate support was provided by several researchers. Crnic, Greenberg, Ragozin, Robinson, and Basham (1983) found significant positive effects on satisfaction with parenting. A positive relationship between kinship social support to mother/female guardians and adolescent psychological and maternal well-being was reported by these researchers. Unger and Wandersman (1988) also found maternal perception of family and partner support to be strongly associated with overall life satisfaction among adolescents. Whether measured prenatally or in the postpartum period, life satisfaction among these women was reportedly quite high at the child's eighth month. Kissman and Shapiro (1990) confirm these findings, suggesting that psychological well-being increases with the availability and size of the family support system.

Other factors have also been influential in determining the personal and social adjustment of teenage mothers. For instance, Barth et al. (1983) found that adolescents' well-being was not only highly correlated with their surrounding social context and the availability of support, but it was also strongly related to the quality of their relationships with their parents. There were more reports of contentment, higher self-esteem, increased locus of control, and less anxiety and depression about life circumstances when mothers were positively reinforced by a supportive social network. Psychological well-being was strongly associated with the level of conflict with parents. In Thompson's (1990) study, female siblings and adolescent peers who seemed to confirm the difficulties and inconveniences of motherhood proved to be sources of stress and distress for new young mothers. Social well-being was most enhanced by support received from a male partner.

When supports are perceived as sources of stress, the likelihood of depressive symptomatology increases. As demonstrated by the work of Barrera (1981), whose study of pregnant adolescents showed that while network size was unrelated to well-being, level of satisfaction with support was a significant predictor of depression and anxiety. Rhodes and Woods' (1995) also found life events and social strain to be positively related to depression in a study of pregnant minority adolescents. Another study, by Rhodes, Ebert, and Fischer (1992), on the role of mentors in countering the potential negative impact of the support networks of African American adolescent mothers showed interactions with network members who provided intangible support were more likely to result in depression among adolescent mothers if the teenagers did not have a mentor in whom they confided regarding stressful life events.

The quality of family relationships has been shown to affect older women coping with the difficulties of parenthood as well. An example of this is illustrated by findings from a study of depression during and after pregnancy (Dimitrovsky, Perez-Hirshberg, & Itskowitz, 1986). A poor relationship with husbands was significantly correlated with depression. If women perceived problems in their marital relations, they were more likely to exhibit depressive symptoms. Depression assessed at pregnancy was also a good predictor of depression during the postpartum period at both 4 and 8 weeks after delivery. Cutrona (1984) reported somewhat different results. Unlike Dimitrovsky and his colleagues, Cutrona found overall support predictive of depression only at later points in the postpartum period (that is, social support was not a predictor of depressive symptoms two weeks after delivery, but it played a significant role in the well-being of new mothers at 8 weeks postpartum).

The absence of specific aspects of social support seemed to be factors most likely to result in depression. For example, in Cutrona's (1983) study, when women perceived deficiencies in their social interactions or a lack of unconditional supports, reports of depression were more likely. However, more positive adjustments were made by others who received support that enhanced their self worth. Women with well rounded support systems (i.e., who received assurances regarding their self-worth, as well as both tangible and intangible support, and who became socially active following the birth of their child) were able to cognitively view the events in their lives as less problematic and less severe. Furthermore, they appeared to have more self-confidence, higher self-esteem, and stronger self-efficacy beliefs. In another study of maternal postpartum depression, the protective function of supportive social relationship was also seen primarily through the mediation of self-efficacy. Less depression and higher levels of self-confidence as parents were reported for women with high levels of social support as assessed prenatally. Although these studies consist of primarily older women (ages 18 to 43), they have important implications for adolescent mothers adjusting to parenthood as well. It has been suggested that maternal self-efficacy mediates the effects on parenting behavior and that it is sensitive to influences of one's social support network (Teti & Gelfand, 1991). Similar results have been reported for teenage mothers who have been found to have a high sense of self-regard, an internal locus of control, and more satisfaction with their parenting role (Colletta & Lee, 1983). Because of the ability of these factors to directly and indirectly affect the developmental outcomes of children, it is essential to understand the ways in which support network members impact upon the parenting practices of adolescent mothers.

Literature Review 25

AVAILABILITY AND UTILIZATION OF SUPPORT

In addition to the mediating effect of the social context surrounding teenage mothers and their children, the availability of an extended support system has also been implicated in the health and developmental outcomes of children born to young mothers. Researchers suggest that the extent to which adolescents are able to adequately perform their parenting duties and to which their children are at risk for poor outcomes depends very much upon the presence of support throughout the pregnancy and child rearing process. According to Whitman, Borkowski, Schellenbach, and Nath (1987), maternal behavior is directly affected by the social support system. Child outcomes, on the other hand, are indirectly affected by the social interactions engaged in by mothers, to the extent to which these interactions enhance the overall quality of parenting.

Theoretical arguments have been made for a direct and indirect effect of the personal social networks of mothers on child outcomes (Cochran & Brassard, 1979). Several researchers have produced results that give credence to this claim. Cooley and Unger (1991), for example, reported that male partner involvement and support from one's own mother resulted in cognitive stimulation in the home. A more direct effect could be seen on measures of vocabulary knowledge and scholastic aptitude, where the mere presence of the grandmother positively related to the test scores. As a consequence of both the direct and indirect influence of social support, the authors witnessed increased achievement scores and fewer child behavior problems. Indirect effects of maternal social support on infant behavior were reported by Crnic et al. (1983). They state that infant social competence is specifically influenced by the support networks of mothers. Crnic, Greenberg, Robinson, and Ragozin (1984) found infant behavior to be positively impacted by maternal support at 4 months postpartum. This effect could not, however, be seen at later periods of assessment. Notwithstanding this, the evidence suggests at least an immediate effect for maternal support.

The negative effects of early parenthood which result in teenage mothers completing less formal schooling, having a lower socioeconomic status (SES), and less unfavorable attitudes toward child rearing have been implicated as correlates of the lack of positive developmental outcomes of their children (Baldwin & Cain, 1980; Roosa, Fitzgerald, & Carlson, 1982a; 1982b). When compared with older mothers, adolescents have been found to provide less opportunity for stimulation, to verbalize less, and to show less affect in their interactions with their children (Jones, Green, & Krauss, 1980; Ragozin, Basham, Crnic, Greenberg, & Robinson, 1982). Garcia-Coll, Hoffman, Van Houten, & Oh (1987) reported that adolescent mothers were less verbally and emotionally responsive to their infants, used more restriction and punishment, and provided less daily variety than adult mothers. A study of 30 primiparous mothers and their full-term infants showed older mothers as more engaging when teaching their infant a specific task (Levine, Garcia-Coll, & Oh, 1985). In comparison to adolescent mothers, older women displayed more positive affect and vocalized more frequently during observations of mother-child interaction. Similarly, Field et al. (1980) found adolescent mothers to be less involved with their children. In fact, adolescents did not look at their infants nearly as often as older mothers. Furthermore, children of young mothers were engaged in activities much less frequently than those of older mothers. The authors categorize the behavioral patterns of teenage mothers as generally unexpressive.

Some researchers have reached the conclusion that the younger the mother, the less responsive and sensitive they are toward their children. For example, McAnarney, Lawrence, Ricuitti, Polley, and Szilagyi's (1986) findings indicated that younger adolescents had a considerably larger number of negative interactions with their children. They were less accessible, accepting, and cooperative with their children. More specifically, a study of 17-24 year-old mothers showed that, compared to mothers 18 and younger, mothers age 19 to 24 demonstrated more responsiveness to their infants. Younger mothers remained distant from and somewhat insensitive to their children. Cooper, Dunst, and Vance (1990) noticed a similar pattern of behavior among mothers less than 16 years of age. After measuring parent-child interaction on separate occasions, results only showed significant increases in the frequency of contingent responses to children's behavior for mothers 16 and older. These findings support earlier reports which suggest that adolescent mothers are less expressive and more harsh in their interactions with their infants.

A number of researchers have concluded that the risk of such negative maternal behaviors among adolescent mothers is considerably greater when these women are isolated from a supportive social network. Social support has been shown to independently effect maternal attitudes and behaviors, and to be associated with increased infant sensitivity and responsiveness (Crnic et al., 1983). Klein and Cordell (1987) identified risk factors among adolescent mothers only to find that the availability of specific forms of social support accounted for differences in the way mothers responded to their infants. Teenagers who received guidance and parenting instruction (either formally or informally) appeared more knowledgeable about the needs of their children, as well as less anxious about and more satisfied with the parenting role. The absence of such support results in adolescent mothers who expressed less satisfaction with parenting and who exhibited a greater tendency toward the use of physical punishment. Infants of these mothers were less likely to be held close enough for effective stimulation or to be smiled at or kissed; their mothers were more likely to be resentful and unappreciative of their children's need(s) for physical contact and stimulation.

Research on the predictors and correlates of anger toward and punitive control of children by adolescent mothers supports findings by Klein and Cordell (1991). In a study of the potential antecedents and correlates of maternal behavior, Crockenberg (1987) reported that low male partner support resulted in more anger and punitive behavior towards children. While no relationship was found between support from one's own mother and maternal behavior in this study, Kissman (1988) did find a correlation between perceived closeness to extended family and punitive and authoritative parenting behavior. Receipt of support and feelings of connectedness with network members enabled young mothers to adopt more positive child rearing attitudes and to incorporate less harsh disciplinary standards.

The notion that the risk of poor developmental outcomes among children of adolescent mothers is related to the level and quality of support by parental social networks was confirmed by several researchers. Colletta (1981) found that the more involved male partners were in the performance of daily tasks, including child care, the less aggressive, rejecting, irritable, and antagonistic adolescent mothers were toward their children. Seymore, Frothingham, MacMillan, and Durant (1990) also found positive effects for mother-child interaction when male partners took part in the care and rearing of the child. Increased paternal involvement was implicated as an essential factor in the enhancement of adolescents' attitudes toward child rearing and in the improvement of the parent-child relationship. The quality of the mother's support network is a clear and consistent predictor of a secure attachment between the young mother and her child (Crockenberg, 1981) and of the home environment (Cooley & Unger, 1991). The type and source of support has been particularly emphasized in the literature, as it is believed that support received from specific significant others is more important than support from a number of other non-significant network members. Perhaps the most crucial sources of support are the extended family and the male partner. It has been postulated that support in the form of emotional concern and functional assistance from these two sources is by far the best predictor of personal and social adjustment among adolescent mothers. A comparative study of Hispanic (English and Spanish speaking) and White adolescents demonstrated this quite effectively (de Anda & Becerra, 1984). Among English speaking Hispanic and White mothers, their own mothers were the most important source of support; husbands and boyfriends served as primary support for Spanish speaking adolescents. In terms of type of support provided most frequently, all adolescents noted the significance of emotional support from their mothers. More functional support from families was received by Whites and English-speaking Hispanics, while their Spanish speaking counterparts depended almost exclusively on male partners for emotional as well as instrumental support.

Unger and Wandersman (1985) illustrate the effectiveness of family and partner support in buffering the stress of early parenting. Emotional support from a male partner was most common; family support, on the other hand, was more closely aligned with the provision of functional and financial support. Kissman (1988) and Kissman and Shapiro (1990) also found adolescents to be receiving functional and financial support most frequently from these two sources. Crnic et al. (1983; 1984) found similar results in two separate studies. Much like results reported by other investigators, the authors found the most positive effect for intimate male support. Support usually took the form of expressions of emotional concern for the adolescent mother's well-being. The factor that differentiated this particular study from other related studies was the role played by community supports. Rather than finding a significant effect for maternal grandmother support, these researchers reported that support from one's surrounding community played a dominant role in the adjustment process as the child grew older. That is, as mothers grew more comfortable with their child care and child rearing responsibilities, they relied less on the support of immediate family members and tapped more into informal neighborhood or community supports (e.g., churches and community centers). Findings from Flaherty, Flaherty, Facteau, and Garver's (1991) study, however, provide continued support for the supportive role of maternal grandmothers. They found grandmothers to be the primary source of support for African American parenting adolescents. Grandmothers provided medical advice, emotional and material support, and child care so that teens could return to school or work. This type of assistance received from both families and male partners has reportedly had the most positive impact on the adjustment of adolescent mothers, as well as on their subsequent parenting practices.

RACIAL DIFFERENCES IN ADOLESCENT SOCIAL SUPPORT

As suggested by previously reviewed data, there are distinct differences in the amount, type, and source of support among adolescent mothers. There is evidence to suggest that such differences also exist across racial lines. Nowhere is that evidence more prevalent than in studies of the intricate support systems of African American families. More specifically, studies have shown African American adolescent mothers to exist within an extended family network where parents, siblings, and other kin (real and fictive) help in the adjustment to the role of parent (Furstenberg & Crawford, 1978; Stack, 1974).

The differential effect of significant others in the lives of African American families has been the subject of both theoretical formulation and empirical investigation (Manns, 1981). Interest in the structure and function of extended family networks in the African American community has led researchers to explore the effects of social support on African American adolescent mothers. Although relatively few studies have been conducted in this area, there is evidence of differences in the social supportnetworks of young mothers from various ethnic groups.

Research indicates that in spite of initial parental disapproval and rejection about pregnancy, African American adolescent mothers experience a marshaling of support from the extended family system. Barth (1988) confirmed this when he reported that the African American adolescent receives a considerable amount of material and other support before and after the birth the child. Barth et al. (1983) compared African American and White adolescents and found the same to be the case. That is, African American teenagers received more of all types of social supportthan their white counterparts. This finding is consistent with those reported by Mayfield-Brown (1989), who investigated the role of family support on low-income adolescent mothers. Also using a sample of African American and White teenage mothers, the author found that members of the former group not only depended on their families more frequently but also received more support from this source than White mothers. Nearly one-half (48%) of African American mothers reported the benefit of family support in the form of housing, financial assistance, and child care as compared with only one-quarter of Whites. The tendency toward a greater dependence on extended family and on higher levels of support can also be seen in results published by Stevens (1988).

Thompson's (1986) examination of the effect of support on adolescents' adjustment to parenthood also shows differences among African American and White teenagers. According to Thompson maternal stress was much higher for White than for African American mothers. Even though African American mothers are less likely to be married (Mayfield-Brown, 1989) and more likely to grow up in disadvantaged neighborhoods and to live under adverse social circumstances (Barnett, 1991; Brooks-Gunn & Chase-Lansdale, 1991), they experience less stress with the responsibilities of mothering than their White counterparts. Thompson (1986) contends that conflicts between traditional values in White families and the increasing proportion of White teens becoming pregnant and opting to parent may force these mothers to live outside their culture, thereby lacking appropriate support.

Low-income Hispanic and African American mothers were investigated to determine ethnic differences in their life experiences (Wasserman et al., 1990a). A considerable proportion of both groups (60% of Hispanics and 79% of African Americans, respectively) reported that they intended to remain in their parents' homes following their deliveries. In addition, they planned to utilize their families as their primary source of support. Nonetheless, differences in the support received were found. For example, Hispanics were much more likely than African Americans to be married and to live with a partner or spouse. On the other hand, African American mothers reported having more support and higher self-esteem. This translated into less restrictive attitudes about child rearing among African American than among Hispanic adolescents. The impact on maternal behavior evident among African American adolescent mothers in Wasserman et al.'s (1990a) study was not substantiated in a similar study by Field,

Widmayer, Adler, & DeCubas (1990). In fact they found just the opposite behavior in this group. A sample of Cuban and African-American adolescent mothers showed more indulgent and engaging behavior among the former group. Cuban mothers were more likely than African American mothers to provide social stimulation for their infants and to exhibit more positive child rearing attitudes. African American mothers, in contrast, maintained more restrictive and punitive attitudes and interacted with the children in less stimulating ways.

Social support, and in particular the extended family network in African American communities, has consistently been shown to mediate the effects of stress. However, some investigators argue that SES plays an equally important role in explaining the variance in maternal psychological distress associated with parenting. Social support alone did not mediate distress in Barth et al.'s (1983) study. Rather, they found the combination of poverty and the absence of supportive social relationships to best predict psychological impairment among young mothers. Similarly, when Turner, Grindstaff, and Phillips (1990) examined maternal stress in relation to one's SES, variations in adjustment outcomes were found. Family support was related to depressive symptomatology among low-SES adolescents. This was true whether teens perceived themselves to be under relatively little stress or whether they reported themselves as overwhelmed by stress. Conversely, family support was found to take on a protective function against the effect of stress for higher-income adolescents.

Mayfield-Brown (1989) contends that the dependence of African American adolescents on the supportive resources of the family has less to do with the amount or quality of their interactions than it does with problems inherent to adjustment to the negative social and economic environments in which they find themselves. In light of the fact that African Americans begin the childbearing process at younger ages, are more likely to remain single, and are less likely to have appropriate coping responses, the need to maintain support systems that facilitate positive adaptation to the parenting role and that sustain adequate parenting attitudes and behaviors may necessarily be challenging and, perhaps, even taxing to the support network itself. This is especially true when one considers that many of the problems these women confront require resolution through financial means. The significance of support in general and, more specifically, of extended family cannot be emphasized enough, as it provides African American adolescent mothers with a means by which to achieve some the tasks of adolescence (e.g., completing high school and preparing for entrance into the workforce) that will result in more encouraging maternal and child outcomes.

EARLY INTERVENTION

Early Intervention programs were initially employed as a strategy to counteract the negative effects of poverty on the development of young children (Brofenbrenner, 1975). The increased risk for low cognitive functioning and subsequent poor school performance has led researchers, as well as health, education, and human service professionals to develop preventive and intervention programs designed to ameliorate the risk of developmental delay of socially disadvantaged children through changes in the attitudes and behaviors of their parents. With the emergence of preventive mental health and maternal and child health as issues of national medical and social concern during the 1970s, early interventions began to diversify to meet the many and varied needs of disadvantaged children and families. It has been hypothesized that early interventions impact upon families in important ways, resulting in substantive and enduring changes in the lives of children and their families (Bronfenbrenner, 1974). This is accomplished through the provision of support that a number of American families appear to be lacking.

The potential for early intervention programs to enhance the attitudes, behaviors, and health practices of mothers and to directly and indirectly improve the developmental outcomes of children cannot be denied. The principles that guide intervention programs have resulted in several key elements that make such programs appealing as measures for addressing the health, educational, social, and emotional needs of families. For example, such programs begin at a formative period in the lives of women and children, extending the concept of primary prevention to the promotion of optimal maternal and child development; they focus on empowering families in ways that enable them to independently establish support systems that continually promote the transactional pattern of parent-child behavior that has been set in motion; and they ensure flexible, accessible, and responsive delivery of services to accommodate the strengths, needs, socioeconomic conditions, or cultural backgrounds of all families (Gray & Wandersman, 1980; Hutchins & McPherson, 1991; Roberts,

Wasik, Casto, & Ramey, 1991; Weissbourd & Kagan, 1989; Zigler & Black, 1989). Nonetheless, questions remain with regard to the ways in which different intervention programs affect family outcome measures. The central question is: which early intervention strategies are most effective in addressing the varying needs of families in different ecological contexts?

While these programs offer a great deal of promise, they have been plagued by methodological problems that have either produced relatively modest or mixed results or resulted in findings that have been difficult to interpret. Some researchers (e.g., Gray & Wandersman, 1980; Halpern, 1984; Olds et al, 1983) argue that decisions made regarding goals, sample populations, comparison groups, outcome measures, and evaluation approaches have involved tradeoffs that affect the strength, range, interpretability, and generalizability of results. Consequently, results of the true effectiveness of early intervention programs have been mixed.

PROBLEMS OF METHODOLOGY

The diversity of early intervention programs seems best evidenced by differences in theoretical and applied issues concerning influential factors in the promotion of positive maternal and child outcomes. In attempts to identify problems commonly encountered by researchers and to explore possible explanations for the lack of program effects, Gray and Wandersman (1980) and Halpern (1984) examined methodological. Several problems were identified as particularly important since they relate to questions of congruence between program goals and the methodological procedures used. These include the definition of goals, the measurement of program effects, and the selection of target populations and comparable controls.

Gray and Wandersman (1980) contend that studies with clearly delineated goals which match available measurement techniques have the best chance of producing positive results. In the past, they argue, goals of the intervention have been broader than their assessment. Problems with a lack of good measures by which to evaluate program effects only further complicates matters. According to Slaughter (1983) and Moran (1985), most research and evaluation on early intervention programs assessed changes in the intellectual development of children, and the only well-developed measures of program outcomes are related to such studies (Weiss, 1988). Bailey and Simeonsson (1988) stress the importance of the selection and use of appropriate measures, pointing out that the use of inadequate measures is a major limitation in the assessment of program effectiveness. It has been suggested that measures be of more than one type. Outcome evaluations must include answers to questions of program effects, provide information on who benefits most from interventions, and determine which types of early interventions work best with which targeted populations.

Decisions about which population to target for services and what constitutes an appropriate control group have also made the evaluation of program interventions difficult. Programs have used an array of approaches to and selection criteria for sampling (Halpern, 1984). Bronfenbrenner (1974) states that inadequate sample sizes and non-randomized trials with local control groups offer researchers fewer design advantages. It is the contention of Olds et al. (1983) that defining appropriate control groups has been made virtually impossible due to unplanned evaluations of program outcomes.

With respect to these limitations, Halpern (1984) offers some possible explanations for the lack of strong quantitative evidence for program effects. Since intervention programs have broadened in scope to include outcome variables besides children's cognitive development, it is difficult to find valid and reliable measures of new constructs, to reach consensus on definitions, and to establish norms for interpreting measures at varying levels of study (i.e., across neighborhoods, communities, regions, etc.). Moreover, small sample sizes may hamper research design by masking program effects. Halpern (1984) formulates a final explanation, echoed by Olds (1990) and Olds and Kitzman (1990), which suggests that early interventions may simply not work in every context or with all populations.

Early intervention programs vary as much in their impact as they do in their goals and the populations targeted, as the following review of the literature demonstrates. The effectiveness of intervention programs on women and children's health and development will be assessed with the general population initially since some studies have samples of both teenage and older mothers. Unfortunately, most such studies fail to report differential impacts of the programs, if any. Consequently, a review of early designed specifically to address issues inherent in adolescent childbearing and child rearing will follow.

EFFECTIVENESS OF EARLY INTERVENTION PROGRAMS

The lack of consistent findings across interventions, as well as the lack of evidence for the long-term effects of such efforts is evidenced by the following studies. Lazar and Darlington (1982) coordinated a follow-up study based on early intervention programs that had sought to improve a number of outcomes for families of preschool children. The researchers wanted to assess the long-range impact of twelve preschool programs. While no differences were found based on sex, race, pretest IQ scores, family size or structure, or maternal education, significant effects were reported for each of these measures years after completion of the program. Program effects showed better achievement scores for children in the experimental group, as well as more positive attitudes and values among these children. Maternal satisfaction with children's school performance was greater when families were involved in an intervention program.

Over time, it appeared as though school performance was mediated by IQ, in some instances, and independent of such scores in others. For example, in cases where the relationship between the intervention and school performance was mediated by IQ, program children with high IQs at age 6 were less likely than controls to be placed in special education classes (5.3% of program children versus 29.4% of controls were placed in remedial courses). However, there were several cases where improvement in school performance was reported for experimental children independent of their IQ scores.

Bronfenbrenner (1975) assessed two types of intervention projects: one which used a center-based setting, and another which employed a home visitor to make regularly scheduled visits to the home to work with women and children. Generally speaking, children who took part in intensive programs of either type showed greater and more enduring gains than controls. More specifically, home visiting resulted in substantial gains in IQ that were still visible several years following the programs. By age 5, however, effects of the intervention could no longer be detected in children's intellectual development. Changes in the attitudes and behaviors of mothers were demonstrated by more positive interactions between women and their children, greater feelings of personal competence, and an internal locus of control.

An important drawback of these studies was the failure to represent all disadvantaged populations due to their lack of participation. By and large, families participating in these intervention programs were on the higher end of the low-income spectrum. Families which endured the most suffering and experienced the most deprivation were too burdened to do much beyond survive from day-to-day.

Support for the lack of participation among highly stressed, low-income families is provided by Unger and Wandersman (1988), who conducted a study specifically designed to examine the factors that influence program participation. Their investigation of prenatal differences among mothers as they related to postpartum participation in a support program showed significant differences based on women's level of active participation and on the availability of social support. Those mothers who actively participated in the program lived with and perceived their families as sources of financial and instrumental support. In addition, they maintained relatively little contact with the baby's father. In contrast, inactive mothers reported intentions to rely on paternal support with child care and financial assistance. When support was not forthcoming following the birth of their children, less stable and more stressful life circumstances were reported for these women. Program participation became understandably inconsistent and unpredictable. The authors emphasize the need for support systems which enable and encourage mothers to take part in service programs. The absence of support makes active participation in intervention programs highly unlikely.

In the preschool programs, the cognitive gains reported during the first year were not as long-lasting as those in home visitation programs. By the second year, and certainly within a year or two after the programs ended, progressive declines were being reported for program children. As decrements increased over time, program children began to more closely resemble controls, who had not experienced substantial improvements in their cognitive development during the initial intervention. Eventually, IQ scores for program children dropped so low as to be considered problematic. This occurred in spite of remarkable gains at earlier stages of the intervention.

Trends similar to those reported for the long-term impact of early interventions on children's cognitive development are also reported by other researchers. The data seem to suggest significant cognitive gains for program children during the early phases of interventions and invariable declines in intellectual development and performance over time. Slaughter (1983) reported this trend in her study of early intervention effects on the educational development of low-income, African American children and their families. Slaughter used two intervention approaches with her sample: 1) a toy demonstration program which involved trained social workers visiting the homes of families twice weekly for a period of two years to engage in model play with children using particular toys; and 2) a discussion group for mothers which met weekly for approximately two hours. A control group was also used for comparison. Project children were found to have considerably higher IQ and verbal scores than control children at 34 and 41 months of age. In fact, the author points out that IQ scores of program children were characteristic of middle income children, while those of the control group reflected the expectations associated with their socioeconomic status and racial group. Unfortunately, Slaughter noticed decrements in the superior cognitive development of children in the experimental group that had begun at 22 months. She suggests that between the ages of 22-41 months, children need additional support in order to continually develop at optimal rates.

Slaughter (1983) also found a similar pattern of program effects for mothers. Differences between program and control mothers showed positive gains for the former group. Program participants interacted more with their children, had higher levels of personal development, and expressed more flexible child rearing attitudes. These gains, reported at the end of the first year of the intervention, were not evident by the end of the second year. At the end of two years, mothers in the program and control groups differed very little in the ways in which they interacted with their children, in their attitudes toward child rearing, and in their feelings of personal competence.

Seitz, Rosenbaum, and Apfel (1985) also confirmed the lack of long-term evidence for children's cognitive development. These researchers examined the cognitive development of 36 children from inner-city communities using an experimental and control group. Families in the former group received home visits (average of 28), pediatric care (13-17 well baby visits and 7-9 developmental screenings), child care (average of 13.2 months), and psychological services tailored to their specific needs from pregnancy through the 30th month postpartum. It was concluded that the principle effects for children were related more to socialization and social adjustment than to enduring cognitive changes. Moreover, improvements were reported only for male children; differences between program and control girls did not approach statistical significance. Whereas control boys were more likely to require school services due to truancy, disobedience, or conflict with other children, program boys were reported to be socially well-adjusted; had better school attendance; and required significantly fewer school services. Although no long-lasting effects were reported for children's intellectual development, Seitz and colleagues (1985) concluded that the family support intervention they employed offered significant potential for long-range improvements in family functioning. Program effects on parents indicated dramatic changes in two areas. Specific to children's development, the authors found program mothers to exhibit a more active interest in the social and intellectual activities of their children. Control mothers, on the other hand, initiated few, if any, contacts with their children's teachers. They also took less pleasure in interactions with their children. Family functioning was also enhanced through increased self-sufficiency over time. Immediate effects for family self-sufficiency could not be detected, yet 10 years after completion of the program virtually all families in the experimental group were self-supporting. Only about half of control families had obtained this same goal. This difference between groups has been attributed to the decreased rate of subsequent pregnancy in program mothers—a factor which increased the chances that women would continue their education or find adequate and stable employment.

The Syracuse Family Development Research Program was conducted to assess the impact of early intervention on low-income children and their families after ten years (Lally, Mangione, & Honig, 1988). The program provided a full range of services to 108 families (predominately African American), including educational, health and safety, and human service resources. The program employed weekly home visits which began prenatally and continued until the children reached elementary school. Much like other researchers, they reported substantial initial gains in the cognitive development and intellectual abilities of children that dissipated as the children grew older. In contrast to Seitz et al. (1985), Lally and associates (1988) found girls to benefit most with respect to school functioning. The effects, they note, were not apparent until the girls reached junior high school; nonetheless, they had better attendance records, higher average grade point averages, and more impressive teacher ratings. Unlike the lack of enduring effects on cognitive changes in children, the higher level of socio-emotional functioning exhibited by program versus control children at 36 months of age was still visible after the program ended.

While Madden, O'Hara, and Levenstein (1984) found some evidence for short-term cognitive effects, there was no indication that the intervention had prevented educational disadvantages by the time the children reached first grade. Children were originally recruited between the ages of 21 and 33 months, with their families being assigned to either a home-based intervention program or to a comparison group. Families in the former group received 46 home visits during the course of each of two school calendar years. In their assessment of three cohorts of families, Madden et al. (1988) reported only modest immediate gains in cognitive development for the first two cohorts (i.e., 1973 and 1974). The third cohort (recruited in 1976) showed more dramatic gains in achievement and IQ scores over the short run. According to results from Wasik, Ramey, Bryant, and Sparling (1990), a marked decline in the intellectual development of low-income children could be seen anywhere between 1 to 1 1/2 to 2 years of age. Using home visitation with infants from 65 families judged to be at high risk for developmental delay due to the social disadvantage of their families, the authors assigned children to one of three groups. Some children were assigned to a control group; others were assigned to an intervention at the Child Development Center, with an additional family education component; a third group of children received only the family education component. Children in the two intervention groups were scheduled to receive weekly home visits for the first three years. Children involved in the intervention reportedly had better measures of cognitive performance than controls. Results of these studies lend support to Halpern's (1984) conclusion that evaluations of the long-range effects of intervention programs are inconclusive.

Other interventions have been designed to assess maternal and child outcomes relative to health. Here, again, the results have been mixed. Perhaps the most notable intervention project in this area is the Prenatal and Early Infancy Program (PEIP), commonly referred to as the Elmira Study (Olds et al., 1986). Beginning in the late 1970s, the study began as a home visiting program providing support to pregnant women, new mothers, and children in one of the most economically disadvantaged communities in the United States. With the goal of ameliorating both social and medical problems that in combination create stressful life circumstances, the program provided trained nurses as supports for a predominantly White sample of more than 400 women and children within the context of their homes on a regular and consistent basis. It was a comprehensive program with evaluations which reflect numerous effects on maternal and child outcome variables. For instance, PEIP was able to assist mothers in obtaining prenatal care, to encourage more appropriate health behaviors among mothers, to improve outcomes in infant birth weight, and to enhance the informal support networks of women in the program.

Moreover, the program was able to effect change in the rates of child maltreatment among single, poor adolescents. In comparison with controls, only a small percentage of these PEIP mothers abused or neglected their children (19% vs. 4%, respectively). A considerable proportion of teens also returned to school, a factor that may have contributed to the decreased rate of repeat pregnancies. Four years after the end of the intervention twice as many unmarried controls as program participants were experiencing a repeat pregnancy. The reduction in the dependence on public assistance may also be attributable to the return to and completion of school among young mothers.

Campbell (1994) contends that the PEIP is one of the most successful interventions not only because its comprehensive approach enables it to affect several of the most critical health problems faced in the US, but also because it is cost-effective. Recently released results of a fifteen-year follow-up of the PEIP, involving 324 of the original 400 women who participated in the study, suggest significant long-term effects of the program as well (Olds, Eckenrode, Henderson, Kitzman, et al., 1997). Study findings revealed positive outcomes for nurse-visited women in general and for poor, unmarried women, in particular. As compared with the control group, nurse-visited women who were unmarried and poor reportedly had fewer subsequent births, with longer periods between their first and second children; were more likely to report fewer arrests and to have state records indicate lower arrest rates; had fewer self-reported behavioral impairments due to alcohol or substance abuse; and were less likely to be receiving Aid to Families With Dependent Children after sixty months as compared to the control groups' average of ninety months. Reports of child abuse and neglect were also significantly lower among women who received nurse visits during pregnancy and infancy than among women in the comparison group.

Another randomized trial of home visitation services yielded equally positive results for the experimental group. Marcenko and Spence (1994) tested the efficacy of home visitation as an intervention strategy for women at risk of out-of-home placement of their newborns. The study used nurses, social workers, and an indigenous home visitor to improve the social support networks and service utilization patterns of inner-city women. A ten month assessment revealed no impact of the program on out-of-home placement or on maternal self-esteem. However, results showed increased social, greater access to services, and decreased psychological distress.

Also using informal social as an intervention strategy, Dawson, Robinson, and Johnson (1982) assessed program effects on parent-child interaction. Home visits were arranged to provide material, emotional, and informational support to mothers from the prenatal period to the child's first year of life. Initial results, obtained at 4 months postpartum, indicated that home-visited mothers were demonstrably warmer in their interactions with their children, and they exhibited greater skill in their parenting practices. Less authoritarian attitudes toward child rearing, more positive maternal behaviors, and increased feelings of personal competence were evident by the end of the project. The program proved most beneficial to select groups, including adolescent, Hispanic, and low-income families.

More recent results from another study of mother-child interaction showed positive outcomes for a predominantly White sample (Kang, Barnard, Hammond, Oshio, et al., 1994). Kang and colleagues employed a multi-site experiment using hospital and home visitation programs to improve interaction between mothers and their newborn infants. Women were grouped by educational level: 1) the high education ((13 years) group was assigned to a hospital intervention and the comparison group to a car seat safety program; and 2) the low education ((12 years) group received a combination of services that included the hospital intervention and the car seat safety programs along with either a pre-term feeding program or standard nurse home visits while the comparison group received only nurse home visits. Although the program yielded no effect at 40 weeks conceptual age, results showed intervention effects on infant behavior (i.e., clearer cues and more vocalizations) during feeding at 1.5 months corrected age for both high and low education groups. Findings at 5 months corrected age, failed to show effects for low education mothers, but effects on interaction among the high education group showed an enduring pattern.

As demonstrated by the Rural Alabama Pregnancy and Infant Health Program (RAPIH) (Nagy, Leeper, Hullett-Robertson, & Northrup, 1992), promising results have not been reported for all intervention studies. The population served in this program was living under severe social and economic circumstances. According to Nagy et al. (1992), the three counties served by RAPIH were at high risk on all counts. The target population was poor African American women, and the goals of the program were to improve pregnancy outcomes and infant health. Home visits, conducted by women selected from the community, were used to provide outreach, education, and social support from the prenatal period until the child's second birthday.

RAPIH was successful in at least two regards, but, overall, the data indicate no effect for the intervention on parenting skill and child development. Although home visited women received prenatal care at later stages in their pregnancies, they made the largest number of prenatal care visits. Most women in the study were reportedly depressed, and while the participation in the program did not reduce the level of depression among women, it did result in enhanced support during labor and delivery. In addition, women in the experimental group were more likely to receive early child care and to ensure that their children received immunizations as scheduled. Participation in the program was associated more with utilization of health care services than with specific maternal and child outcomes.

Dawson, Doorninck, and Robinson (1989) reported results that were quite similar. To enhance mother-infant interaction among a sample of low-income women, paraprofessional home visitors provided emotional and informational support to mothers during pregnancy and throughout the infants' first year. A disproportionate number of infants received health care, but no significant differences were found between the treatment and control groups in perinatal outcomes for mothers. Furthermore, the two groups did not differ significantly on any of the outcome measures included in the intervention to assess maternal and child health.

Findings by Siegel, Bauman, Schaefer, Saunders, and Ingram (1980) suggest much the same thing. Where some studies have at least been able to report program effects on health care utilization, such was not the case with these researchers. The support intervention was designed to impact maternal and child health and development through several outcome measures. These researchers used an early and extended contact approach with 321 women in their third trimester of pregnancy. Early contact consisted of a minimum of 45 minutes of mother-infant interaction contact during the first three hours following delivery and five additional hours on each of the remaining days in the hospital. Extended contact involved paraprofessional home visitors meeting mothers during their hospital stay and following-up with each of them at home nine times over the course of the first three months of the children's lives. On the whole, the intervention was not effective in improving the outcomes for women and children. More specifically, Siegel et al. (1980) found no significant effect for the intervention on maternal attachment, utilization of health care services, or reductions in reports of child maltreatment. The positive impacts on mother-child interaction that were witnessed were attributed to background variables, which the authors contend explained a significant amount of the variance in maternal behavior.

The potential of early intervention programs to promote change in the health and development of women and children is what drives many researchers who design, conduct, and evaluate such programs. This is true irrespective of the age at which childbearing takes place. Nonetheless, the relative importance of such strategies increases dramatically when the targeted population is adolescent mothers and their offspring. With data to suggest that adolescents fail to engage their infants in ways that facilitate optimal growth and development, the need to evaluate intervention programs designed to eliminate or minimize the deleterious effects of early parenting on mothers and children is paramount. As with interventions for the general population of women and children, there appears to be considerable variance in the impact of programs on maternal and child outcomes among adolescents and their offspring.

EARLY INTERVENTION FOR ADOLESCENT MOTHERS

To evaluate the effects of a home-based, parent training intervention program for pre-term infants of low-income, African American teenage mothers (<19 years), Field et al. (1980) compared the infants' development to that of non-intervention controls (consisting of term infants of teenage mothers) and of term and pre-term infants of adult mothers. Participants received bi-weekly home visits that provided education, infant stimulation exercises, and assistance with positive mother-child interactions. Results revealed that pre-term infants who received intervention had greater weight and length measures and higher developmental scores at 4 months of age than infants in the control group. At 8 months, their Bayley mental scores were significantly higher than scores for the control infants.

While teenage mothers, as a group, were generally found to have less optimal attitudes and perceptions than their adult counterparts, intervention mothers were reportedly more likely to express realistic expectations for child development and to show more desirable child-rearing attitudes at 4 months. In addition, women in this group received higher ratings for face-to-face interaction at 4 months and higher Caldwell ratings for emotional and verbal responsiveness and maternal involvement at 8 months. Ratings of infants' temperament (at 4 and 8 months) were considerably more positive among intervention mothers than among controls.

Thompson, Cappleman, Conrad, & Jordan (1982) also found evidence in favor of early intervention for young, poor, African American mothers and their children. Results from a monthly nurse visiting program designed to enhance children's developmental functioning and mother-child interaction during the first two years of life showed that both mothers and children benefited. There were variations in the interaction patterns between mother and infants as a function of the intervention and the children's level of developmental risk. Nonetheless, intervention mothers were more likely than mothers in the control group to praise and provide positive feedback to their children and to be less restricting. In addition, they directed their children less and were able to provide less help to children. Their children, in turn, were found to be more cooperative than control group children.

At 2 1/2 years, intervention children had IQ scores that were an average of 8.45 points higher than those of children whose mothers were in the control group. The difference, albeit non-significant, provided support for the finding that half (50%) of controls remained at risk for cognitive delays at 30 months of age as compared to only 11% of children who had the intervention.

Using a largely African American and Hispanic sample of 14-19 year old adolescent mothers living in a residential maternity home, Koniak-Griffin and Verzemnieks (1991) evaluated the impact of a nursing intervention program on maternal role attainment. A significant increase in maternal-infant attachment scores over time were reported for mothers assigned to the intervention group. While not statistically significant, these women were also more likely than controls to score high on the measure which assessed maternal-fetal interaction activities. This was true for the total score as well as for subscales.

Unfortunately, higher scores were not reflective of more positive mothering behavior for these mothers as compared with controls.

Several researchers have found positive effects of intervention studies on maternal behavior. Early work by Badger, Burns and Rhoads (1976) reported improvements in maternal behavior among a sample of 225 African American and White inner-city adolescent mothers recruited to participate in a hospital-based education program. The program consisted of more than 30 hours of class time (appropriately 18-20 sessions) over a 12-month period. Unlike other intervention programs, mothers were not actively involved until their children were 6 months of age. Nonetheless, mother-infant interaction was shown to increase over time. Mothers were increasingly more responsive to the needs of their infants, while infants' responses toward their mothers also improved.

Gutelius, Kirsch, MacDonald, Riddick-Brooks, and McErlean (1977) also reported improvements in the parenting behaviors of adolescent mothers. Gutelius and colleagues used an intensive 3-year child health supervision approach with 47 African American infants of low-income, inner-city, single adolescent mothers to enhance parenting behavior. A sample of forty-eight infants of teenage mothers were used as a comparison group. The program offered child health supervision, counseling, anticipatory guidance, and cognitive stimulation through home-visits of approximately once per month. A combined total of 18, 12, and 8 visits were made respectively over the course of the three years.

A number of positive effects were reported using this approach. For example, children in the experimental group were found to have better diets and eating habits than children in the control group. At age 3, significantly more experimental than control children scored high on six of 14 characteristics from the Stanford-Binet Intelligence test. Differences were also visible at age 4, with experimental children displaying more confidence and assurance. Finally, mothers involved in the intervention were significantly more likely than control mothers to report their children as less problematic at age 5 (58% as compared with 31%, respectively) and age 6 (79% versus 54%).

In addition to finding greater familial and financial stability among experimental women, they were also reported to have increased levels of confidence and security fostered by the intervention. More importantly, improvements in the way mothers interacted with their children were found. By 2 years of age, the rate at which intervention mothers engaged their children in conversation reached significance. Likewise, substantially more women in this group than in the control group were reportedly handling their children's fussiness in developmentally appropriate ways.

Findings by Landy, Schubert, Cleland, and Montgomery (1984) further highlight the importance of early intervention. Landy and colleagues evaluated the impact of an early intervention program on 14 teenage mothers' and the subsequent impact on their children's development. The study employed two contact groups—one with teenage mothers and their infants, and the other with women over 20 years of age (N=12)—and a non-intervention control group. Contact groups were tested and observed an average of 11 times during the course of a year but received no structured intervention.

While the children of adolescents were not found to differ dramatically from those of older women, significant differences were reported for intervention mothers versus non-intervention controls. A significant intervention effect was found for infant development, mother-child attachment, and the home environment. Infants whose mothers had the intervention scored higher on both the motor and mental scales of the Bayley. Unlike the mothers in the experimental group, control mothers engaged in less adequate interactions with infants, including hitting them or ignoring their crying. Furthermore, controls engaged in less face-to-face interaction with their infants and talked to them less than did contact group mothers. Contact group mothers not only interacted in more positive ways with their infants, but they also provided better home environments for them.

Employing a slightly different approach to improving outcomes for young mothers and their children, Field, Widmayer, Greenberg, and Stoller (1982) compared a home-visit, parent-training program and a nursery parent-training intervention program to a non-intervention control group provided for a select group of 120 low-income, African American teenage mothers (13-19 years of age). Women were randomly assigned, in equal numbers, to one of the three groups. Home-visited mothers received bi-weekly visits in infant stimulation during the first six months of the infants' life. During the same six month period, mothers assigned to the nursery group received paid job training by working 4 hours per day as teacher aides in a medical school nursery. They received the same parent-training as home-visited mothers, as well as had direct exposure to modeling of child care techniques from nursery staff members.

Developmental assessments of infants at 4 and 8 months of age revealed that infants receiving the intervention weighed more and were rated as having less difficult temperaments than those in the control group. Their pattern of superior weight sustained itself through the second year of life, with higher Bayley motor and higher mental and motor scores at one and two years of age, respectively.

While general findings revealed overall positive effects for women receiving the intervention as compared with those in the control group, nursery intervention mothers seemed to benefit slightly more than did nurse-visited mothers. Videotapes of mother-child interaction showed intervention mothers talking to the infants much more than did controls, and their infants seemed to be engaging them at a much higher rate. The number of mothers who returned to school during the first year was far greater among those receiving the nursery intervention than those assigned the home visits. Moreover, nursery intervention mothers were less likely than home-visited mothers to experience a repeat pregnancy within the first year of motherhood.

Not all studies of the impact of early interventionson adolescent mothers and their children have not yielded such positive results. For example, in the Adolescent Parents Project, Miller (1992) found little or no impact on prenatal care and child outcomes among young mothers. The intervention was carried out in two locations: Atlanta and Toledo. Participants were very young (15 years old or less), poor, and predominantly African American. The principal effects were realized only for the Atlanta sample and only with regard to health related behaviors. Teenage mothers reported more frequent postpartum clinic visits and fewer health problems for themselves and their children. Similarly, Olds (1984) reported unsuccessful efforts in improving the quality of maternal care giving in his study of prenatal and postpartum nurse home visitationfor high-risk families. While the intervention was able to improve child health and development in a number of cases, there were instances in which improvements in the qualities of maternal care giving were unsuccessful. Using case studies of several low-income, single adolescent mothers, Olds (1984) discussed factors that interfered with nurse home visitors' ability to enhance maternal care giving.

As the literature on the short-term, immediate effects of early intervention on maternal and child development indicate, the impact of individual program interventions vary and are sometimes not effective at all. Mixed results are also common with regard to the long-term effects of such programs. In fact, as a result of the relatively small number of studies with teenage samples which investigate the enduring effects of program interventions, the results of such studies are much less clear than those on the immediate impact of social interventions. This is illustrated by the difference in findings reported by Gray and Ramey (1986) and Stone, Bendell, and Field (1988). Gray and Ramey (1986) conducted a study of 14 low-income, African American women who had participated in an intervention during their preschool years. At the time of their study, the women were in high school and had given birth to their first child. Assigning 8 mothers to an experimental group and 6 to a control group, the investigators assessed the impact of an early training program on the rate of high school completion among the young mothers. They found the experimental group to have a significantly higher graduation rate, to have more stable family lives, and to receive more support from family members than controls. This, in turn, resulted in higher levels of motivation and more competent achievements.

Stone and colleagues (1988) used a subsample of 61 mother-child dyads to investigate the impact of an intervention program on school performance. Children (ages 5-8 years), born to teenage mothers, were randomly assigned to experimental (N=31) and control groups (N=30). Nineteen of the intervention mothers had received nursery-based training, while 12 had been trained in their homes. Short-term effects of the intervention program had been witnessed, but there were no lingering effects of the intervention for mother or child at 5 to 8 years following its completion.

Despite the paucity of studies of the long-range benefits of support interventions, findings from the above studies consistently point to positive outcomes for mothers and children. The fact that intervention programs offer potential for affecting change make them encouraging strategies for addressing the needs of families with children at risk for adverse developmental outcomes. McDonough (1984) contends that the short-term effect on the attitudes, knowledge, and interactional behaviors of adolescent mothers has been significantly positive, even though the long-term impact of postpartum interventions remains unclear. Panzarine (1988) argues that the challenge is not only to determine how long these positive benefits last, but also to understand the mechanisms by which they occur.

Literature Review

SUMMARY

Problems of methodology notwithstanding, the literature seems to suggest that early intervention programs provide a positive impact on various aspects of maternal functioning for older and younger mothers alike. Although some studies of the effectiveness of intervention programs have yielded mixed results—usually attributed to problems of methodology—the majority of those focusing on adolescents have consistently reported significant, positive effects for the intervention group as compared with non-intervention controls. The paucity of evidence for the long-range effects of early interventions suggests the need to develop strategies that provide mothers with knowledge and skills which stand the test of time. The extent to which this can be accomplished will add greatly to our understanding of the mechanisms used to sustain the beneficial effects of intervention programs for mothers and their children.

CHAPTER 3
Methodology

OVERVIEW

This chapter describes the sampling procedure, the data and their limitations, and the method of analysis used in the present study. Because the present study is based on a subset of cases drawn from a larger study, it is first necessary to provide some background information regarding the original study.

BACKGROUND

The current study is a secondary analysis of data collected during the late 1970's and early 1980's for the Prenatal/Early Infancy Project (PEIP). The PEIP was a randomized clinical trial of prenatal and postnatal nurse home visits for socially disadvantaged families in a semi-rural community in upstate New York. Designed to improve pregnancy and child rearing outcomes, the PEIP included the provision of medical and transportation services, as well as nurse home visits, through the children's second year of life. Evaluation procedures were conducted throughout this period, and a follow-up study was conducted when the children were 3-4 years old to assess long-term program effects on maternal and child health and development.

Women bearing their first child were recruited for the study if they also had at least one of three characteristics predisposing their infants to health and developmental problems: young age (less than 19 years); single-parent status; and low socioeconomic status (SES). A sample of 400 women was enrolled in the PEIP prior to their 30th week of pregnancy. Participating families were randomly assigned to one of the following treatment conditions:

51

Treatment 1: Families in this group received no services. However, at 1 and 2 years of age, infants underwent sensory and developmental screening to detect problems. Children with suspected problems were referred to specialists for further evaluation and treatment.

Treatment 2: Families in this group also received sensory and developmental screening. In addition, provisions were made through a contract with a local cab company for free transportation to prenatal and well-child visits at clinics and physicians' offices.

Treatment 3: A nurse-home visitor was provided to families during pregnancy, in addition to screening and transportation services. Nurses made bi-weekly visits of approximately one hour and 15 minutes each, with an average of nine visits.

Treatment 4: Families assigned to this group received nurse home visits throughout their pregnancies and until their babies reached 2 years of age. Nurse visits occurred weekly during the month immediately following delivery, with regular visits of diminishing frequency over time. Between the 18-24 month period of the infants' lives, visits were made at six-week intervals.

While nurse home visits were tailored to the specific needs of each family, nurses were responsible for accomplishing three major tasks: 1) to educate women about fetal and infant development; 2) to enhance the informal support available to women during pregnancy, birth, and subsequent early child rearing; and 3) to link families with community-based health and human services.

PRESENT STUDY

In light of the literature on the consequences of early childbearing for both mother and child, it is imperative that early intervention programs be assessed to determine their ability to enhance the natural support systems of young mothers with children. The purpose of this study was to investigate the impact of the PEIP on social support for adolescent mothers. Interest in the differential role of social support for African American and White adolescent mothers was the primary motivation behind this research. The questions that guided this research were as follows:

1. Does the PEIP enhance the natural support systems of young mothers?
2. If so, how does that vary as a function of race?

While this study does not address the bigger question of whether social support improves the child rearing behaviors of adolescent mothers, it does take the first step in addressing this question by examining the differential impact of a comprehensive early intervention program on the social support networks of African American and White adolescents. Investigating the role of social support among adolescents from different racial groups will aid in filling some of the gaps in the literature on social support, particularly as it relates to social interventions designed to ameliorate or prevent adolescent pregnancy. In this way, new information is available about racial differences in social support that may be used to create more effective interventions and programs that meet the needs of specific populations.

SAMPLE AND PROCEDURE

A sample of 141 women possessing all three risk characteristics—i.e., they were young, single, and poor—was drawn from the PEIP data set for inclusion in the present study. The definition of adolescence was expanded here to be consistent with the notion of maternal readiness, which suggests that the optimal time for childbearing is between the ages of 22-31 (Ragozin, Basham, Crnic, Greenberg, & Robinson, 1982). Consequently, mothers in the sample ranged in age from 13-21 years. All women were unmarried at the time of the intervention and fell into Hollingshead's social classes IV and V (semiskilled and unskilled laborers). Values less than 59 were indicative of these social classes.

The decision to conduct the present study with only poor, unmarried, teenage mothers was based on results of the original PEIP study. Findings from the original study suggest that program interventions with single, poor women appear to be more effective than those with other subgroups. By focusing exclusively on this group, the present study stands to offer valuable insight into the ability of a comprehensive early intervention program to enhance the support networks of a group of women known to potentially experience stressful life circumstances due to the identified risk factors of age, marital status, and economic stability.

Unlike the original study, the present study sample was composed of both African American and White adolescents. Published findings from the original study of the PEIP did not include non-White cases. These cases were excluded from all analyses because sample size (N=46) was too small to provide adequate subclass sizes when included in the statistical model with other important factors (Olds et al., 1986). In contrast, African American women fitting the specified criteria for the current study were included in all analyses. Eighty-four percent of the present study sample were White (N=118) and 16% were African American (N=23).

COMBINING TREATMENT GROUPS

Treatment groups 1 and 2 were combined for purposes of analyses, as they were in the original study. They comprised the control group and accounted for 46% (N=65) of the sample. Due to the paucity of African American cases in the data set, it was also necessary to combine treatments 3 & 4. This group was referred to as the nurse-visited group, without distinction being made with respect to duration of visits (i.e., whether they were prenatally only or throughout pregnancy and the child's second year of life). Fifty-four percent (N=76) of the sample were assigned to the nurse-visited group. African American mothers accounted for less than 20% of cases irrespective of treatment condition (14% in the control group, and 18% in the nurse-visited group). Estimates of treatment differences were based on the contrast between women who received nurse home visits and those who did not. Due to the possible confounding effect of the child's birth weight, it was controlled in all analyses.**Error! Bookmark not defined.**

SOCIAL SUPPORT OPERATIONALIZED

Analyses of these data were conducted using social support as the dependent variable, and treatment group assignment as the independent variable. Measures of social support were based on assessments taken upon entrance into the PEIP (intake), at the 8th month of pregnancy, at the hospital following labor and delivery, and at 6, 10, and 22 months of the child's life. Since the study focused on the amount of support received—anticipated or actual—social support was coded on a three point scale, where 1=little or no support, 2=some support, and 3=a lot of support. Where necessary, due to a relatively small number of cases

Methodology

in any one of the above categories, categories were redefined in the following manner: little/none, little/some, some/a lot, and a lot. Table 3.1 outlines support variables and assessments used in the study.

As the literature illustrates, the social support construct has been conceptualized in various ways. In the present study, social support was used primarily to measure functional/instrumental support.

Analyses were restricted largely to measures of this particular type of support, as most of the available data were of this nature. However, a measure of emotional support was also included in the study. Where data were available, information about the source of support was also provided.

Functional/instrumental support included the amount of help expected from or provided by the support person(s) with child care responsibilities and domestic chores. Emotional support was assessed using a variable that gauged the level of support person interest in the pregnancy and, subsequently, in the child. While this type of support was based on only one variable, it was measured at each point in time. The exception was during the hospital stay, where the focus was on support person's assistance with labor and delivery, as well as their reaction and response to the child following its birth. These reports of social support were based on the observations of hospital maternity nurses. Maternity nurse ratings of social support during labor and delivery were based on the presence or absence of support persons, which were recorded as "yes" or "no." To determine the extent to which support persons interacted with the newborn, nurses used four scales on which support person behavior was rated as little/none or some/a lot. The scales were designed to assess support person behavior by using a combination of variables. They were as follows: Scale 1 measured extent to which the infant was held, explored, or looked at; Scale 2 evaluated support person's emotional reaction to the newborn, as well as the amount of time spent holding or talking to the infant; Scale 3 examined the extent to which the infant was explored and talked to; and Scale 4 measured the amount of holding and exploring behaviors, as well as the amount of time spent talking to infants.

In an attempt to evaluate the effect of the PEIP on actual support, data from the 6, 10, and 22 month periods were grouped for the child care, domestic help, and interest [in the child] variables. This resulted in a measure of overall support for each of the functional support activities and a measure of the level of interest in the child over time.

Persons identified by respondents as their primary sources of support were categorized into three groups: 1) male partner, which included support from a boyfriend or other male who may or may not have been the father of the infant; 2) family, which included support from the respondent's own mother, other family members, or the family as a whole; and 3) other, which included support from any number of other sources ranging from the boyfriend's family to friends to no one at all. The categories are consistent with the literature, which suggests that the most salient sources of support are the maternal grandmothers of infants and male partners of respondents.

METHOD OF ANALYSIS

The study employed simple descriptive statistics and multiple regression for analyses of these data. Descriptive statistics and correlations have been conducted to evaluate the distributional characteristics of the variables, as well as to investigate the directions and strengths of relationships between variables [produced using SAS]. Results of the correlations indicate that support variables were marginally to significantly related to one another (from .10 to .70). Multiple regression was also employed to test the relationship between PEIP, race, and social support. To do this, I first wanted to test the direct effects of race and the PEIP on outcome variables. Secondly, and perhaps more importantly, I wanted to examine the moderating effect of race on PEIP and social among African American and White adolescents.

Cross-tabulation procedures were also employed to determine estimates of poor, unmarried teenage mothers as a function of treatment condition and race. Chi-square statistics were used to test the null hypothesis of independence between the variables of interest. Although the analysis procedure yielded three different chi-square statistics, the results presented from the present study are based on the Pearson chi-square statistic.

Methodology

Table 3.1. Support Variables

Variable Label	Assessment Period
Labor/Delivery	Intake
Labor	Hospital
Delivery	Hospital
Reaction to & Level of Interaction with Infant (assessed using four scales)	Hospital
Child care	Intake 6 months 10 months 22 months
Chores	Intake 8 months of pregnancy 6 months 10 months 22 months
Husband/boyfriend Interest	Intake 8 months of pregnancy 6 months 10 months 22 months
Source of Support (assessed for labor/delivery, child care, & chores)	Intake

LIMITATIONS OF THE DATA

Some caveats must be expressed about these data. The major limitation of this study arises from using secondary data. It was very difficult to reconstruct the variables used by Olds and colleagues because precise records had not been kept to document them. While the PEIP offered a wealth of valuable data, there was no code book available to identify variables or to clarify the time period at which specific variables were assessed. Variables were identified by matching labels assigned in the data set with response options from questionnaires used in the original study. When this method failed to produce appropriate variables for this study, identification and clarification was provided by the Principal Investigator (PI) of the PEIP. In light of the number of years that have passed since the study was conducted, coupled with poor documentation, the PI found it necessarily difficult to recall specific variable codes and to identify variables at each time period.

This problem was experienced with particular frustration with respect to variables that contained information on the identification of support person(s). Since variables were not consistently labeled in a way that clearly indicated what they measured, it was impossible to locate all of the variables containing information about who respondents identified as their support person for each task at each point in time. As a consequence, data about who provided support were only available for the intake period. Being unable to address the question of who the source(s) of support was for young mothers was an unfortunate drawback given the paucity of studies that have investigated racial/ethnic differences in the social networks of adolescent mothers.

Appropriate cautions aside, the study attempts to add further understanding to the impact of social interventions on the natural support systems of adolescent mothers. In so doing, it seeks to address the policy implications of similar types of programs in the hope of providing information that will help to increase the effectiveness of policies and agencies which attempt to ameliorate or prevent adolescent pregnancy.

CHAPTER 4
Results

OVERVIEW

The study employed simple descriptive statistics, correlations, cross-tabulations and multiple regression for analyses of these data. Results presented below are based on two types of evidence: 1) cross tabulations were used to test bi-variate relationships and 2) a single, step-wise linear regression model was employed to control for effects of other variables and to test interactions between treatment condition and race. The regression model was used to predict social outcomes using sociodemographic, as well as baseline data as control variables. Infants' birth weight, race, treatment group status, and a treatment group x race interaction term were included in the model for each analysis. Baseline data are reported here, independent of subsequent support. However, intake differences were controlled for when looking at treatment effects later. That is, when predicting specific types of support outcomes, baseline data were included as control variables when appropriate.

There is one cautionary note regarding regression analyses presented herein. Due to the relatively small sample size represented in the present study, results of these analyses may not have been sensitive to differences in the sample. It is possible that this factor may have effected the power of the statistical approaches employed herein to yield more fruitful results. Results of both the regressions and the cross tabulations are presented by treatment group and by race.

ANTICIPATED CHILD CARE AND CHORE SUPPORT

Results of contingency table analyses are shown in Table 4.1. Poor, unmarried nurse-visited adolescent mothers were significantly more likely than mothers in the control group to report high rates of anticipated support for child care at intake ($p<.01$). Fifty percent of mothers in the nurse-visited group expected that they would receive support with child care responsibilities. A disproportionate number (71%) of control group adolescents reported little or no anticipated support with child care. Regression analyses, conducted to predict anticipated support for child care, revealed a marginally significant effect for treatment group condition (beta=.13, $p<.10$) when controlling for race and a race x treatment interaction.

Table 4.1 also shows significant treatment group differences between African American and White adolescent mothers on anticipated support with the care of their children once born. For example, White mothers assigned to home visits were significantly more likely than those in the control group to expect assistance with the care of their children at intake ($p<.05$). Nearly half (47%) of nurse-visited White mothers anticipated some or a lot of support, while only 29% of White teenagers without home reported the same.

A similar trend was found with regard to chore support at intake among poor, unmarried White adolescent mothers receiving home visitation, reaching significance at $p<.05$. Ninety-five percent of nurse-visited adolescents reported high levels of anticipated support with chores. In contrast, White teenagers assigned to the control group were more than three times more likely than nurse-visited, White mothers to expect that their support person would provide minimal support with domestic chores (18% as compared with 5%, respectively). Results of the regression model confirmed these findings, with significant independent effects for treatment group status (beta=.28, $p<.01$) and for race (beta=.20, $p<.12$).

By the 8th month of pregnancy, a shift had taken place along treatment group status and racial lines. Control group adolescents were found to be considerably more likely than their nurse-visited counterparts to report expectantly high levels of support with chores at the 8th month of pregnancy (83%. vs. 71%, respectively). Among poor, unmarried African American adolescents, disproportionately more women in the control group than in the nurse-visited group felt that they would receive assistance with household chores. The

Results

overwhelming majority (89%) of controls anticipated a lot of such support compared with only 57% of nurse-visited adolescent mothers.

These findings were marginally significant, with p<.10, using contingency table analyses. Regression analyses revealed that the treatment x race interaction term was a significant predictor of expected support during pregnancy, although not in the expected direction (beta=-.36, p<.01). This suggests that the effect of the treatment varied as a function of race, with poor, unmarried African Americans teens assigned to the control group being much more likely than adolescent mothers assigned home visitation.

Table 4.1. Anticipated Child Care and Chore Support, by Treatment Group and by Race

Dependent Variable	Group	Anticipated Support	
		little/none	some/a lot
Child Care (intake)			
	**Nurse-visited (N=76)	50%	50%
	Controls (N=65)	71%	29%
African Americans	Nurse-visited (N=14)	36%	64%
	Controls (N=9)	67%	33%
*Whites	Nurse-visited (N=62)	53%	47%
	Controls (N=56)	71%	29%
Chores (intake)	Nurse-visited (N=76)	05%	95%
	Controls (N=65)	15%	85%
African Americans	Nurse-visited (N=14)	07%	93%
	Controls (N=9)	00%	100%
*Whites	Nurse-visited (N=62)	05%	95%
	Controls (N=56)	18%	82%
Chores (@ 8 mo/preg)	Nurse-visited (N=76)	29%	71%
	†Controls (N=65)	17%	83%
African Americans	Nurse-visited (N=14)	43%	57%
	†Controls (N=9)	11%	89%
Whites	Nurse-visited (N=62)	26%	74%
	Controls (N=56)	18%	82%

**p<.01   *p<.05   †p<.10

ANTICIPATED VERSUS ACTUAL LABOR/DELIVERY SUPPORT

Treatment Group Differences. The percentage of poor, unmarried adolescent mothers in both the nurse-visited and the control group who anticipated and actually received support during labor and delivery is presented in Table 4.2. It should be pointed out that support for labor and delivery was measured jointly at intake. Each was, however, measured independently once mothers arrived at the hospital to give birth. In addition, anticipated support was measured with regard to amount of support mothers thought they would receive during labor/delivery, whereas measures of support at the hospital were based on its presence or absence as recorded by hospital maternity nurses. Anticipated support will be discussed as it relates to the entire labor/delivery process; findings for support during actual labor and delivery are presented independent of one another.

Table 4.2. Perceived Versus Actual Labor/Delivery Support, by Treatment Group

Dependent Variable	Group	Anticipated Support little/none	some/a lot
labor/delivery	Nurse-visited (N=74)	15%	85%
	Controls (N=56)	11%	89%
Support Received at Hospital		Yes	No
labor	*Nurse-visited (N=58)	97%	03%
	Controls (N=57)	86%	14%
delivery	Nurse-visited (N=56)	32%	68%
	Controls (N=56)	23%	77%

*p<.05

As indicated by Table 4.2, anticipated labor/delivery support was more closely associated with labor support than with support during delivery. The amount of anticipated support for labor/delivery was relatively equal across and within groups, with nearly 90% of all poor, unmarried adolescent mothers expecting that they would receive some or a lot of support. The difference between mothers in each group who received support for labor upon reaching the hospital was significant (p<.05). Results of these analyses show that 97% of poor, unmarried nurse-visited mothers were reported to have been accompanied to the labor room by a support person. More than three times as many poor, unmarried control group than nurse-visited mothers were reported to experience labor alone (14% vs. 3%, respectively). A similar result was found when employing the regression model (beta=.9, p<.05).

Race Differences. Significant group differences in anticipated labor/delivery support, as a function of race, were not evident in the analyses conducted (See Table 4.3). A significant difference was detected, in both types of analyses, among White adolescents in the nurse-visited group during actual labor at the hospital (p<.10). Ninety-six percent of controls from this group received support while in labor with their child; in contrast to only 86% of White control group teenagers.

Although not a significant finding, Table 4.3 does show a general trend toward higher levels of anticipated and actual support received among poor, unmarried adolescents exposed to treatment conditions. This was true without regard to race. The exception to this was found among White control group mothers relative to delivery support. For this particular group of mothers, the inverse situation was true with respect to actual support received during delivery. Adolescents assigned to the control group were found to be accompanied to the delivery room on a slightly more frequent basis than adolescents assigned nurses (75.5% as compared with 63%).

Table 4.3. Perceived Versus Actual Labor/Delivery Support, by Race

Dependent Variable	Group	Anticipated Support	
labor/delivery		little/none	some/a lot
African Americans	Nurse-visited (N=14)	21%	79%
	Controls (N=8)	12.5%	87.5%
Whites	Nurse-visited (N=60)	13%	87%
	Controls (N=48)	10%	90%
Support Received at Hospital			
labor		Yes	No
African Americans	Nurse-visited (N=10)	100%	0%
	(Controls) (N=7)	86%	14%
Whites†	Nurse-visited (N=50)	96%	04%
	Controls (N=48)	86%	14%
delivery			
African Americans	Nurse-visited (N=10)	90%	10%
	Controls (N=7)	86%	14%
Whites	Nurse-visited (N=46)	63%	37%
	Controls (N=49)	75.5%	24.5%

†p<.10

SOURCE OF ANTICIPATED SUPPORT AT INTAKE

As mentioned in Chapter 3, data were, unfortunately, not available on the sources of support upon which poor, unmarried teenagers relied after the birth of their child. Findings are reported here only for source of support information available at intake. While analyses yielded no significant group differences, irrespective of treatment condition or race, this information is believed to provide valuable insight into the people upon whom young women rely as they make the transition to motherhood.

Treatment Group Differences. There was little difference in the proportion of nurse-visited and control group mothers who expected assistance from male partners on all types of support. Table 4.4 reflects the general trends between the two groups. As illustrated, the trend for anticipated source of support is such that poor, unmarried adolescents

Results

in the nurse-visited condition were somewhat more likely than adolescents in the control group to identify male partners as primary support persons for labor/delivery and child care. Conversely, women in the control group condition tended to report an anticipated reliance on family members across all types of support.

Well over half of poor, unmarried adolescent mothers expected support from male partners during labor/delivery (58% of controls and 59% of nurse-visited mothers, respectively) and for child care (51% of controls and 56% of nurse-visited mothers, respectively). Far fewer adolescent mothers in both groups reported expected male partner support with chores.

When compared to reports of anticipated support from male partners for labor/delivery and child care, there were relatively few mothers, irrespective of treatment condition, who expected their husband/boyfriend to help with household chores. Roughly a quarter (27% in the control group and 22% in the nurse-visited group) of poor, unmarried adolescents reported that they expected the assistance of their male-partner with chores. The majority of adolescent mothers in both the control and nurse-visited groups indicated that their families would be the sources of support on which they relied most heavily for support with household responsibilities.

Table 4.4. Source of Support at Intake, by Treatment Group

Dep. Variable	Group	Husb/Bf	Family	Other
labor/delivery	Nurse-Visited (N=76)	59%	36%	05%
	Controls (N=59)	58%	37%	05%
child care	Nurse-Visited (N=72)	56%	39%	06%
	Controls (N=55)	51%	47%	02%
chores	Nurse-Visited (N=76)	22%	65%	13%
	Controls (N=60)	27%	67%	07%

Another interesting difference of note is the degree to which each group expected support from persons other than family members or male partners. The proportion of adolescents in either group who indicated their intended reliance on support from a source other than their husband/boyfriend or their family was exactly the same for labor/delivery. Nurse-visited mothers tended to report anticipated support from "other" sources two to three times more often than control group participants.

Race Differences. The treatment group differences by race were not significant for source of support, as illustrated in Table 4.5. Without regard to treatment condition, poor, unmarried White teenagers were much more likely than their African American counterparts to report support from "other" sources. No African American teenager identified persons other than their families or male partners as sources of support as they made the transition to motherhood. Relatively equal proportions of poor, unmarried teenagers in both racial groups were represented in each category for source of support for labor/delivery. Approximat 'y half of poor, unmarried African American teenagers, irrespective of treatment condition, reported that they expected the help of both their husband/boyfriend and their family during labor/delivery. Approximately 60% of poor, unmarried White teenagers (in th~ nurse-visited and control group) reported that their husband/boyfriend would be their primarily source of support during labor/delivery. A similar proportion of poor, unmarried White adolescents also expected support from this source for child care (62% among nurse-visited teenagers and 50% among controls, respectively).

Family support was more frequently reported by African American mothers in both treatment groups than by White mothers. Sixty-three percent of controls and 58% of nurse-visited teenagers in this group expected family support with household chores. The proportion of poor, unmarried White adolescents who believed their male partners would help them with chores dropped to just over 25% (26% for nurse-visited and 29% for control group mothers).

Support from the teenagers' own family was expected to increase after the birth of their children for poor, unmarried African American teenagers. Disproportionately more African American nurse-visited adolescents expected the support of their families with child care and chore support. Seventy-one percent of those who received home visits stated that they expected family members to assist them with child care responsibilities as compared with only 44% of controls. All but 7% of nurse-visited, African American teenagers responded this way with regard to chore support.

Table 4.5. Source of Support at Intake, by Race

Dep. Variable	Group	Husb/Bf	Family	Other
labor/delivery				
African Americans	Nurse-visited (N=14)	50%	50%	0%
	Controls (N=9)	44%	56%	0%
Whites	Nurse-visited (N=62)	61%	32%	07%
	Controls (N=50)	60%	34%	06%
child care				
African Americans	Nurse-visited (N=14)	29%	71%	0%
	Controls (N=9)	56%	44%	0%
Whites	Nurse-visited (N=58)	62%	31%	07%
	Controls (N=46)	50%	48%	02%
chores				
African Americans	Nurse-visited (N=14)	07%	93%	0%
	Controls (N=9)	11%	89%	0%
Whites	Nurse-visited (N=62)	26%	58%	16%
	Controls (N=51)	29%	63%	08%

COMPARISON OF INTEREST IN PREGNANCY WITH INTEREST SHOWN IN CHILD

Unlike other support variables, level of interest was assessed for husband/boyfriend only. Thus, all responses are based on adolescents' assessment of the amount of interest their partners expressed in their pregnancies and in their children at 6, 10, and 22 months of life.

Treatment Group Differences. The overall level of husband/boyfriend interest in the pregnancy appeared to be associated with subsequent interest in the child for nurse-visited, as well as control group, mothers. Table 4.6 shows that the percentage of mothers in both groups that reported a lot of male partner interest in the child was larger than the proportion who experienced a similar level of interest in their pregnancies. The difference in the percentage of mothers who reported high levels of husband/boyfriend interest in their pregnancies and whose partners also showed a lot of interest in their children over time was most visible among nurse-visited mothers. When comparing findings at each assessment period, the difference between the nurse-visited and control groups was most obvious when children were 6 months old. The difference between the level of husband/boyfriend interest in the infant at the 6th month of life was highly significant (p<.001). Virtually all (97%) of those in the nurse-visited treatment group rated interest levels extremely high. Nearly one-third (32%) of poor, unmarried teens in the control group reported male partner interest low to moderate compared with only 6% of adolescent mothers receiving nurse home visits. The number of controls reporting low levels of male partner interest was almost six times as many that in the nurse-visited group.

Generally speaking, poor, unmarried adolescents in the nurse-visited and control groups were not significantly different from one another at the 10 or 22 month assessment periods. Nurse-visited mothers were, however, consistently more likely than mothers in the control group to report male partners who expressed a lot of interest in their pregnancies and in their children over time. Reports of high levels of husband/boyfriend interest among controls remained relatively stable up through the children's 10th month of life. Reported interest among control group male partners seemed to peak at 22 months, with slightly more than three-quarters (79%) of adolescents in this group feeling that their partners were very interested in their children.

Regressions were run on all of the above interest variables, with significant results for husband/boyfriend interest at 6 and 22 months. In the model predicting interest at 6 months, there was a main effect for interest at intake (beta, p<.05) such that level of husband/boyfriend interest at intake predicted the level of interest in the child at 6 months of life. Likewise, when predicting interest at 22 months, a significant main effect was found for husband/boyfriend interest at 6 months (beta=.51, p<.001).

Results

Table 4.6. Husband/Boyfriend Interest in Pregnancy as Predictor of Interest in Child, by Treatment Group

Time Period	Group	Interest in Pregnancy	
		little/some	a lot
Intake	Nurse-visited (N=70)	29%	71%
	Controls (N=53)	40%	60%
8th month	Controls (N=56)	34%	66%
of Pregnancy	Nurse-visited (N=56)	33%	67%
		Interest in Child	
		little/some	a lot
6 months	***Nurse-visited (N=47)	06%	97%
	Controls (N=44)	32%	68%
10 months	Nurse-visited (N=43)	26%	74%
	Controls (N=45)	31%	69%
22 months	Nurse-visited (N=47)	17%	83%
	Controls (N=52)	21%	79%

***$p<.001$

Race Differences. There were significant and interesting variations across treatment conditions as a function of race (see Table 4.7). Poor, unmarried, African American adolescents assigned a nurse were more likely than their control group counterparts to report male partner interest in their pregnancies at intake (83% vs. 75%). There was a considerable increase in the proportion of nurse-visited mothers reporting little or no interest at 8 months of pregnancy. No African American nurse-visited teenagers had rated interest as little or some at intake, yet 22% described the amount of interest in their pregnancies as such when they were in their 8th month. The proportion of African American teenagers in the control group whose partners showed a lot of interest in their pregnancy increased from 75% at intake to 89% when they were 8 months pregnant.

Treatment group differences in the amount of interest shown in the child were significant at 6 and 10 months for poor, unmarried African American teenagers ($p<.01$ and $p<.05$, respectively). Disproportionately more nurse-visited than control group teenagers had male partners who expressed interest in their children. Half of the African American teenagers assigned as controls rated interest in child as little or some; no nurse-visited teenagers were found to have such uninterested partners. Women assigned home visits were much more likely than those in the control group to report high levels of interest in their children.

Whites in the nurse-visited group were more likely than their counterparts in the control group to report interested partners at intake, at 8 months of pregnancy, and at 6 and 22 months of the child's life. As with the African American nurse-visited group, results showed interest in the child at 6 months of age to be significant. Disproportionately more nurse-visited than control group mothers had husbands/boyfriends who were very interested in their children at 6 months. Ninety-two percent of White teenagers receiving nurse-visits reported a lot of interest in their children; only 70% of treatment control teenagers rated interest this way.

Results from the regression model confirmed those findings presented above, as well as provided additional information. For example, an interaction effect for treatment x race was found when predicting male partner interest at 6 months (beta=.38, p<.06). As demonstrated by the data in Table 4.7, poor, unmarried adolescents receiving home visits, both African American and White, were more frequently reported as having partners with high levels of interest in their children. Regression analysis showed husband/boyfriend interest at 6 months to significantly predict level of interest in child at 10 months (beta=.41, p<.001). When using the model to test for main effects at 22 months, interest at 6 months was again found to be a significant predictor (beta=.51, p<.001). In addition, a significant main effect for race was also found (beta=.33, p<.05). These findings suggest that African American nurse-visited mothers had an increased likelihood that husbands/boyfriends would show greater interest in their children.

Results

Table 4.7. Amount of Husband/Boyfriend Interest in Pregnancy as Predictor of Interest in Child, by Race

Time Period	Group	Interest in Pregnancy	
Intake		little/some	a lot
African Americans	Nurse-visited (N=12)	17%	83%
	Controls (N=8)	25%	75%
Whites	Nurse-visited (N=58)	31%	69%
	Controls (N=45)	42%	58%
8th month/pregnancy			
African Americans	Nurse-visited (N=9)	22%	78%
	Controls (N=9)	11%	89%
Whites	Nurse-visited (N=43)	35%	65%
	Controls (N=47)	38%	62%
		Interest in Child	
6 months		little/some	a lot
African Americans**	Nurse-visited (N=11)	0%	100%
	Controls (N=4)	50%	50%
Whites**	Nurse-visited (N=36)	08%	92%
	Controls (N=40)	30%	70%
10 months			
African Americans*	Nurse-visited (N=9)	11%	89%
	Controls (N=6)	67%	33%
Whites	Nurse-visited (N=34)	29%	71%
	Controls (N=39)	26%	74%
22 months			
African Americans	Nurse-visited (N=10)	10%	90%
	Controls (N=7)	14%	86%
Whites	Nurse-visited (N=37)	19%	81%
	Controls (N=45)	22%	78%

**p<.01 *p<.05

REACTION TO CHILD AT BIRTH AND SUBSEQUENT SOCIAL SUPPORT

Immediately following the birth of the child, the level of interaction each support person had with an infant, as well as his/her emotional response to the infant, was observed by maternity nurses at the hospital. Four scales were developed, each measuring 2-3 items. Scale 1 assessed the extent to which support persons held, explored, and looked at the infant; scale 2 measured their emotional reactions, as well as the amount of time spent holding and talking to the newborn; scale 3 examined the extent to which infants' bodies were explored and they were talked to; and scale 4 evaluated the same items as scale 3, along with support persons' level of interest in holding the baby.

To determine the extent to which maternal nurse observations of support person behavior predicted future support, a comparison was made with adolescent mothers' self-reports of child care and chore support when their children were 6, 10, and 22 months of age. Each type of support will be discussed in turn, with emphases on treatment group and racial differences at each time period, where appropriate. No significant group differences were found, irrespective of treatment condition or race.

Treatment Group Differences. The overwhelming majority of support persons in both groups were reported as having less than positive reactions to infants or as engaging infants only rarely in interactions. Nurses were more likely to rate support person behavior as interactive for mothers in the home-visited group than their counterparts in the control group. Between 13% and 17% of support persons for the nurse-visited group were reported as having positive interactions with newborns on all scales as compared with only 8% to 11% of controls.

As Table 4.8 indicates, maternal nurse observations of support person behavior were not very reflective of the amount of support adolescents received with child care and chores. In general, nurse-visited adolescent mothers were more likely than controls to report some or a lot of support for child care responsibilities. In contrast to reports for child care which favored nurse-visited mothers, controls were found to be more likely than their nurse-visited counterparts to experience support for chores. The difference between the levels of support received with chores among control and nurse-visited mothers reached significance at the 6 month assessment ($p<.05$), with poor, unmarried adolescent mothers in the control group considerably more likely than women in the home-visited group to report receiving a lot of support with household chores (46% as compared with 30%, respectively).

Results

To further test these support variables, regressions were run to predict support outcomes at 6 and 22 months. Main effects for chore support at intake (beta=.18, p<.05) and for treatment condition (beta=-.18, p<.05) were found when predicting chore support at 6 months. The first result suggested that anticipated support for chores was a significant predictor of the amount of chore support women reported receiving at 6 months. Although not in the expected direction, the latter finding showed that poor, unmarried adolescents assigned to the control condition made more frequent reports of high levels of chore support. A similar regression conducted for chore support at 22 months revealed that chore support at 6 months was a significant predictor of the amount of support adolescent mothers received at 22 months.

Race Differences. Maternal nurse ratings of positive support person behavior were much more likely to favor the supports of poor, unmarried White adolescents, especially those in the nurse-visited treatment group (see Table 4.9a). Poor, unmarried White teenagers were found to have the behavior of their support persons rated much more highly than was the case for poor, unmarried African American teenagers. Treatment group assignment was not a determining factor.

Within the White group, results show nurse-visited mothers as the more frequent recipients of positive support person behavior ratings. Between 14% and 19% of the support persons of poor, unmarried White nurse-visited teenagers were believed to engage in the activities on each scale. This was in contrast to only 9%-12.5% of support persons for White control group mothers.

Table 4.8. Reaction to and Level of Interaction with Infant as Compared with Child Care and Chore Support Over Time, by Treatment Group

Scale	Group	Reaction/Response to Newborn	
		little/none	some/a lot
Scale 1	Nurse-visited (N=76)	83%	17%
	Control (N=65)	89%	11%
Scale 2	Nurse-visited (N=76)	85%	15%
	Control (N=65)	92%	08%
Scale 3	Nurse-visited (N=76)	87%	13%
	Control (N=65)	89%	11%
Scale 4	Nurse-visited (N=76)	85%	15%
	Control (N=65)	92%	08%

Support Type	Group	Social Support	
Child Care		little/none	some/a lot
6 months	Nurse-visited (N=76)	82%	18%
	Control (N=65)	80%	20%
10 months	Nurse-visited	74%	26%
	Control (N=65)	71%	29%
22 months	Nurse-visited (N=76)	71%	29%
	Control (N=65)	78%	22%
Chores	Nurse-visited (N=76)	70%	30%
6 months	*Control (N=65)	54%	46%
10 months	Nurse-visited (N=76)	59%	41%
	Control (N=65)	52%	48%
22 months	Nurse-visited (N=76)	78%	22%
	Control (N=65)	71%	29%

*$p<.05$

Support person behavior was rated positively more often for poor, unmarried, nurse-visited African American teenagers than for those assigned as treatment controls. While 7% of nurse-visited African American teenagers were reported to have a support person whose interaction with the newborn on all scales was rated highly, no such observations were reported by maternity nurses for mothers in the control group.

Results 75

Table 4.9a. Reaction to and Level of Interaction with Infant, by Race

Scale	Group	Response to Newborn	
Scale 1	little/none some/a lot		
African Americans	Nurse-visited (N=14)	93%	07%
	Controls (N=9)	100%	0%
Whites	Nurse-visited (N=62)	81%	19%
	Controls (N=56)	87.5%	12.5%
Scale 2			
African Americans	Nurse-visited (N=14)	93%	07%
	Controls (N=9)	100%	0%
Whites	Nurse-visited (N=62)	84%	16%
	Controls (N=56)	91%	09%
Scale 3			
African Americans	Nurse-visited (N=14)	93%	07%
	Controls (N=9)	100%	0%
Whites	Nurse-visited (N=62)	85.5%	14.5%
	Controls (N=56)	87.5%	12.5%
Scale 4			
African Americans	Nurse-visited (N=14)	93%	07%
	Controls (N=9)	100%	0%
Whites	Nurse-visited (N=62)	84%	16%
	Controls (N=56)	91%	09%

Observations by hospital maternity nurses did not generally appear to correlate highly with the level of support poor, unmarried adolescents received after the birth of their child. Worthy of note, however, is the parallel between maternity nurse ratings for African American support persons and the percentage of African American nurse-visited adolescent mothers who reported receiving a lot of support with the care of their children at 6 months. As shown in Table 4.9b, only 7% of mothers in this group received support with child care responsibilities—the exact same percentage that hospital maternity nurses recorded as having supportive and interactive network members. In fact, control group mothers were more than five times more likely to report high levels of child care support than mothers assigned to home visitation. The contrast between one-third (33%) of controls and only 7% of nurse-visited adolescents rating child care support in this way was marginally significant ($p<.10$).

With respect to chores, poor, unmarried African Americans in the control group were found to receive more help from members of their support networks. Nearly seventy percent (67%) of mothers in the control group reported a lot of support for household chores at 6 months as compared with 50% of nurse-visited adolescent mothers. As in the above instance this findings was note highly significant, but instead marginally significant (p<.10).

Among poor, unmarried White teenagers, maternity nurse ratings seemed to be more closely aligned with child care support than support with household chores. Teenagers assigned to nurse-visits were found to receive child care support more frequently at 6 and 22 months than were adolescents in the control group. Results for chore support indicate that teenagers assigned to treatment control conditions were more likely than those in the nurse-visited group to receive help during the first two years of their children's lives. The most visible difference can be seen among African American mothers at the 22 month assessment period. Significantly more poor, unmarried African American adolescents in the control group (56%) were receiving support with household chores than was the case with nurse-visited African American mothers (21%) at this point in their children's development (p<.10).

Using the regression model described earlier, analyses were conducted to predict child care and chore support, controlling for selected baseline variables and demographic factors. The only relevant significant findings were related to chore support at 6 and 22 months, where a marginal effect for treatment group assignment x race was detected (beta=-.22, p<.10) and a highly significant main effect was found for chores at 6 months (beta=.28, p<.001). This finding adds further credence to that reported earlier from Table 4.9b, which suggests that African American adolescents assigned to the control group condition were more likely than their African American or White nurse-visited counterparts to receive assistance with domestic chores.

SUMMARY

The data presented here seem to suggest that there are some effects for the PEIP, even though the evidence was not always strong and in the expected direction. It appears as though considerable differences existed between treatment and control groups, as well as between White and African American adolescent mothers. Table 4.10 shows a chronological summary of significant main effects by treatment group and race.

As the table indicates, nurse-visited mothers were much more likely than their control group counterparts to expect that they would receive high levels of support with child care and household chores. However, only African American control group mothers were found to actually receive significant levels of such support. More specifically, results show that African American adolescents in the control group reported more support for chores at the 8th month of pregnancy and at the 6 and 22 month assessments than African American or White mothers in the nurse-visited group. Significant levels of child care support were also found for this group when their infants were 6 months of age. It was the case that adolescents in the treatment group were accompanied to labor much more frequently than adolescents in the control group. In addition, treatment group mothers reported significantly greater levels of husband/boyfriend interest in their child at 6, 10, and 22 months. Differences by race suggest that African American adolescents in the nurse-visited group were more likely to experience consistent male partner interest over time, with reportedly high levels of interest at each of the postpartum assessment periods. White adolescents in the same group were found to have higher expectations for tangible support at intake and to experience more support during labor. Explanations for these findings and the implications they have for policy formulation, as well as recommendations for future research, will be discussed in Chapters 5 and 6.

Table 4.9b. Child Care and Chore Support Over Time, by Race

Child Care	Group	Social Support	
6 months		little/none	some/a lot
African Americans	Nurse-visited (N=14)	93%	07%
	†Controls (N=9)	67%	33%
Whites	Nurse-visited (N=62)	79%	21%
	Controls (N=56)	82%	18%
10 months			
African Americans	Nurse-visited (N=14)	79%	21%
	Controls (N=9)	67%	33%
Whites	Nurse-visited (N=62)	73%	27%
	Controls (N=56)	71%	29%
22 months			
African Americans	Nurse-visited (N=14)	71%	29%
	Controls (N=9)	78%	22%
Whites	Nurse-visited (N=62)	71%	29%
	Controls (N=56)	79%	21%
Chores Support			
6 months			
African Americans	Nurse-visited (N=14)	50%	50%
	†Controls (N=9)	33%	67%
Whites	Nurse-visited (N=62)	74%	26%
	Controls (N=56)	57%	43%
10 months			
African Americans	Nurse-visited (N=14)	43%	57%
	Controls (N=9)	33%	67%
Whites	Nurse-visited (N=62)	63%	37%
	Controls (N=56)	55%	44%
22 months			
African Americans	Nurse-visited (N=14)	79%	21%
	†Controls (N=9)	44%	56%
Whites	Nurse-visited (N=62)	77%	22%
	Controls (N=56)	75%	25%

† $p<.10$

Table 4.10. Chronological Summary of Significant Main Effects, by Treatment Group and Race

Time Period	Support Type	Nurse-Visited Moms
Intake	Chores	White moms (p<.05)
	Child care	Entire sample (p< .01)
		White moms (p< .05)
Hospital	Labor	Entire sample (p<.05)
		White moms (p<.10)
6 months	Husb/bf interest	Entire sample (p<.001)
		African American moms (p<.01)
		White moms (p<.01)
10 months	Husb/bf interest	African American moms (p<.05)
22 months*	Husb/bf interest	Entire sample (p<.001)
		African American moms (p<.05)

Time Period	Support Type	Control Group Moms
8 months of pregnancy	Chores	Entire sample (p<.10)
		African American moms (p<.10)
6 months	Child care	African American moms (p<.10)
	Chores	Entire sample (p<.05)
	Husb/bf interest	African American moms (p<.10)
22 months	Chore support	African American moms (p<.10)

*based on regression analysis only

CHAPTER 5
Discussion

OVERVIEW

Results of this secondary analysis of data, drawn from the Prenatal/Early Infancy Program (PEIP), show some evidence of positive program effects with regard to enhancing the natural support systems of poor, unmarried African American and White adolescents. Significant positive effects of the program were found in the present study, although not always in the expected direction. Statistically significant findings were also reported as a function of race. The pattern of findings was interesting even if there was a lack of significant main effects for the program over time. Explanations for all findings will be offered here.

The findings presented in Chapter 4 are somewhat consistent with the hypotheses put forth in Chapter 1. It was believed that effects of the program on social support would be moderated by race such that differences between groups would be found as a function of race. Some reported findings were not consistent with the stated hypotheses. It is of note that results of the present study differ from those reported for the PEIP. This is due in large part to the differing goals of and approaches used in each study. While this study, like the PEIP, focused on women at highest risk for problems—i.e., poor, unmarried adolescents—the outcome measures of each study were different.

The PEIP measured maternal health habits, infant care giving, and personal accomplishments in the areas of work, education, and family planning among older and younger White mothers. The program was found to improve the conditions and outcomes of pregnancy and to reduce the incidence of care giving dysfunction most noticeably among families at greatest risk for particular problems in these areas (Olds, Henderson, Chamberlin, & Tatelbaum, 1988). In contrast, the present study examined the impact of the program on the social networks of poor, unmarried African American and White teenagers. Furthermore, outcome variables were measured quite differently.

To the extent that some of the reported findings from the PEIP focused on the social support networks of poor, unmarried teenagers, there was some consistency in findings. Unfortunately, there appears to have been very little overlap in the two studies with respect to measures of social support since the PEIP did not focus specifically on outcomes in this area. That is to say, there was virtually no overlap in analyses conducted in the present study and that of the PEIP (Olds et al., 1988). It was not the intent of this study to replicate findings from the PEIP but rather to examine its impact on an aspect of adolescents' lives shown to influence their adjustment to the mothering roleConsequently, the present study was not conducted with all of the same variables used in the PEIP.

IMPACT OF TREATMENT CONDITION ON SOCIAL SUPPORT

Although significant main effects of the program were found, there appeared to be a paucity of evidence for a main effect of the program on women after the birth of their children. Results do not show a great deal in terms of an independent effect of the PEIP on women in statistically significant and consistent ways over time. The exception was husband/boyfriend interest, for which program effects were found over time for all nurse-visited mothers (irrespective of race).

Nurse-visited, poor, unmarried teenagers were found to be receiving significantly more support from members of their networks prior to the provision of services than were their control group counterparts. For example, nurse-visited mothers reported considerably higher rates of anticipated support for child care ($p<.01$) and chore support ($p<.05$) at intake than did their control group counterparts. (The latter finding was true for poor, unmarried White teens but did not apply equally to African American adolescents.) Olds and colleagues (1988) caution that such pre-intervention differences may have been associated with other conditions which biased the sample in unknown ways. This was highly likely in the present study since, unlike Olds et al., no statistical adjustments were made to account for this difference between nurse-visited and control group teenager mothers.

While there is no way to accurately account for differences between groups at intake, at least two other explanations are possible. First, it is likely that knowledge of involvement in the study led to increased expectations on the part of nurse-visited mothers. That is, the treatment may have had an unintended effect on mothers that resulted in women in this group expecting that with treatment they would necessarily have high levels of support over the course of the study. Alternatively, it is possible that these are merely random effects. This unexpected difference between treatment and control group mothers suggests the need for further exploration and research.

The first actual impact of the PEIP was found for labor support at the hospital. Adolescents assigned to the nurse-visited group tended to be accompanied to the labor room far more frequently than controls ($p<.05$). Virtually all (97%) nurse-visited, poor, unmarried adolescents were accompanied to the labor room. Almost five times as many control group teenagers than nurse-visited adolescents went through labor alone (14% as compared with 3%). White adolescents, in particular, were found to have a support person with them during labor much more frequently than were African American adolescents in the same group. Support for White mothers in the treatment group reached significance at $p<.10$. While this finding may be an artifact of pre-intervention differences in the level of support received by nurse-visited and control group adolescent mothers, it is more likely the case that receiving home visits designed to educate young women and members of their support network about healthy maternal and child outcomes played an important role in support received during labor. This finding is consistent with that of Olds and colleagues (1988), who reported that poor, unmarried teenagers exposed to the program were found to have much higher rates of support during labor than adolescents who received no services.

There was only one significant main effect of the early intervention program on poor, unmarried adolescent mothers over time. Contingency table analyses as well as multiple regression procedures revealed significant findings in support of the PEIP with regard to male partner interest. It was found that husband/boyfriend interest in children at 6 months of life was significantly predicted by treatment group condition ($p<.001$) and level of male partner interest at intake ($p<.05$). That is, it appears as though being assigned to the nurse-visiting condition increased the likelihood that male partners would take a more active interest in the newborns. The level of interest expressed prior to delivery (i.e., in the pregnancy) seemed to predict the level of husband/boyfriend interest at the child's sixth month of life. A treatment x race interaction term was entered into the regression model to test for an interaction effect. That information, while pertaining to the results presented here, will be discussed in connection with the results of effects by race.

A host of other, albeit non-significant, differences were found between adolescents in the two groups. By and large, findings in support of the program favored nurse-visited, poor, unmarried mothers. Mothers in this group were more likely to report that they expected their primary source of support to be their husbands/boyfriends for all types of support; to have male partners who expressed more interest in their pregnancies, who interacted more frequently with their newborn infants, and who showed a lot of interest in their children during the first two years of life; and to receive more help with child care responsibilities.

The increased likelihood that nurse-visited mothers would expect to rely on support from their husbands/boyfriends confirms findings by Olds and colleagues (1988). They reported that the number of nurse-visited, poor, unmarried teenagers supported by their boyfriends at intake exceeded that of mothers in the control group. Thus, it stands to reason that the level of anticipated support from male partners would be greater among this group than among controls. Other findings for the nurse-visited group seem best explained by the effects of the program, even if they were not significant. It would appear that having nurse home visits that encouraged the participation of relatives and male partners would lead to reports of more support from this group than from poor, unmarried teenagers in the control group. Nurses were charged with the responsibility to encourage support person participation in the home visits, as well as to encourage support through attending childbirth classes, acting as coaches during labor and delivery, and helping with household chores. Provided that mothers in this group are known to have more boyfriend support, it would not be unrealistic to expect that, along with encouragement from visiting nurses, male partners would show high levels of interest in the pregnancies of adolescents, engage the newborn in interactions, and demonstrate continued interest in the child as s/he grew older.

Discussion

Notwithstanding the more general positive findings for nurse-visited, poor, unmarried adolescents, there were interesting findings for adolescents in the control group. For example, poor, unmarried adolescents in the control group were found to report higher levels of support with chores at the 8th month of pregnancy than their counterparts in the nurse-visited group. Eighty-three percent of women in the former group as compared with 71% in the home visiting group indicated that they anticipated a lot of support with household chores after the birth of their child ($p<.10$). In addition, results of regression analyses revealed that adolescent controls received significantly more support with domestic chores at the 6 month assessment than did adolescents receiving home visits ($p<.05$). Although not statistically significant, poor, unmarried adolescents in the control group were also more likely to anticipate the support of family members rather than husbands/boyfriends or other persons than their nurse-visited counterparts.

Anticipated and actual support received with household chores and the reliance on family members for all types of support among poor, unmarried adolescents in the control group is consistent with findings reported by several researchers (Furstenberg & Crawford, 1978; Schilmoeller et al., 1991; Thompson, 1991; Unger & Wandersman, 1988; Wasserman et al., 1990b; Zuckerman et al., 1979). Adolescent mothers have frequently been found to remain in their parents' homes after the birth of their child and to rely heavily upon their parents for emotional, psychological, instrumental, and financial support. Mayfield-Brown (1989) argues that teenage mothers tend to depend on the support of their immediate or extended families due to limited options. She contends that adolescents' young age and limited formal education make competing in the labor force difficult, if not impossible.

Family members have been reported to assist adolescent mothers considerably after the birth of their child. Consistent with findings on adolescents' dependence on family support are reports that suggest that the help control group mothers reported with chores are the logical extension of living in their parents' homes. Household responsibilities have likely been delegated before the occurrence of pregnancy among adolescents, with family members contributing somewhat equally to their completion.

THE MODERATING EFFECT OF RACE ON SOCIAL SUPPORT
Anticipated Support for Labor/Delivery, Child Care, and Chores

Results from pre-intervention measures reveal that poor, unmarried White teenagers assigned a nurse were significantly more likely to anticipate support with child care and household chores (p<.05) than were their counterparts in the control group. Nearly half (47%) of all teenagers assigned home visitation reported anticipated support for child care, while 95% expected to receive support with household chores. This finding would seem to be attributed to the fact that husband or boyfriend support among White teenagers in the nurse-visited group exceeded that of their control group counterparts prior to the provision of services. It makes sense that if nurse-visited teenagers felt as though they were supported during the early stages of their pregnancies, their rates of continued support would necessarily surpass those of controls who had already reported less support from members of their network.

The significantly larger number of poor, unmarried African American teenagers in the control group (p<.10) who expected to receive a lot of support with household chores at 8 months of pregnancy, chore support at 6 and 22 months, and assistance with child care at their children's 6 months of life is perhaps more difficult to explain. Close to 90% (89%) of African American adolescents in the control group expected to receive a lot of support with household chores at 8 months of pregnancy in contrast to 57% of women in the nurse-visiting group. The percentage difference between African American mothers in the nurse-visited and control groups was also dramatic with respect to child care at 6 months. One-third (33%) of controls as compared with only 7% of nurse-visited African American adolescents reported receiving a lot of support with child care responsibilities. Not quite as dramatic were findings for chore support at 6 months. Here, 67% versus 50% of the women in the respective groups indicated that they received assistance with chores. By the 22 month assessment, 56% of controls as compared with less than a quarter (21%) of nurse-visited mothers were reportedly receiving help with household chores.

As mentioned, in spite of initial parental disapproval and rejection about pregnancy, African American mothers experience a marshaling of support from the extended family system. Barth (1988), Barth et al.

Discussion

(1983), Mayfield-Brown (1989), and Stevens (1988) have found that African American adolescents not only depended on their families more frequently but also received more support from this source than White mothers. With that in mind, it could be argued that African American adolescents in the control group underestimated the level of support they would likely receive due to the reactions to the news of their pregnancies. According to Thompson (1986), the initial reaction of the parents of African American adolescents is less than positive. The fact that support network members rallied around African American adolescents in the present study once the child arrived and remained consistently helpful over time is in keeping with reports from the above researchers.

It is also conceivable that as the date for delivery approached, the need to prepare the home physically for the arrival of the child could have prompted increased support for chores. This would be particularly true if adolescent mothers were living with their parents. The level of expected support with household chores would naturally increase if assistance had begun to be provided with such tasks in anticipation of the child's birth. This, too, is consistent with reports from other researchers.

An explanation of the reason(s) why similar results were not found for African American adolescents in the nurse-visited group may simply be that the support network believed that adolescents' involvement in the intervention precluded their involvement. That is to say, members of the support network may have assumed that involvement in such a project served the function of family or other support. Or, at the very least, was a vehicle through which adolescents could learn how to manage the responsibilities of motherhood independently. If this were true, it would make sense that support for child care and chores was visibly absent while male partner interest increased. If, in fact, it is the case that family members largely provide these forms of support, the absence of it could well be the result of family members wanting to encourage independence among young mothers.

In so doing, family members may have played a secondary role to husbands or boyfriends with respect to being involved in home visits. That would certainly help to explain the high levels of interest in children among male partners. The lack of evidence for tangible male partner support over time may be interpreted as a premature goal in light of the relatively high level of absent teenage fathers and the fact that most young mothers reside with their parents (and expect their support first and foremost).

Pre-Intervention Source of Support

The person upon which poor, unmarried teenagers said they relied at intake and anticipated continued support from after the birth of the child was included for analysis even though it was the only available information on source of support for the present study. While measuring source of support at this stage alone does not allow for accurate information about who the actual sources of support were for teenage mothers, it is valuable information in that it provides insight about who makes up the support networks of pregnant adolescents. As mentioned earlier, data on source of support could not be located in the larger data set when identifying variables for inclusion in the present study.

Despite the shortcomings of this aspect of the study, the results of analyses on anticipated support were consistent with findings reported by other researchers (e.g., Mayfield-Brown, 1989; Stevens, 1988).

Poor, unmarried African American teenagers expected support for labor and delivery to come from male partners and family members. Approximately half of mothers in both the nurse-visited and the control group expected support from husbands/boyfriends while the other half reported an anticipated reliance on family members. During this time, there is a need for tremendous encouragement and emotional support. Findings by Unger and Wandersman (1985) suggest that emotional support from a male partner is a very common predictor of adolescents' adjustment to motherhood. Crnic et al. (1983; 1984) found similar results in two separate studies. Much like results reported by other investigators, the authors found intimate male support to be salient and to take the form of expressions of emotional concern for the adolescent mother's well-being.

Family support, while also important to the labor/delivery process, is often times more closely aligned with the provision of functional and financial support (Unger and Wandersman, 1985). Findings from the present study support this. Poor, unmarried African American mothers, regardless of treatment group status, were more likely than their White counterparts to expect greatest support from family members after the birth of their child. This was the case with both child care and household chores, where a disproportionate number of African

Discussion

American teenage mothers indicated the importance of their families in adjusting to parenthood (71% for child care and 93% for chores). Barth (1988), for example, reported that the African American adolescent receives a considerable amount of material and other support before and after the birth the child. Another study by Barth et al. (1983) comparing African American and White adolescents found that African American teenagers received more of all types of social support than their White counterparts.

Also of note among poor, unmarried African American teenagers was the fact that none of them (no matter which treatment group they were assigned) identified their anticipated source of support as "other." This makes perfect sense when one considers that studies have shown African American adolescent mothers to exist within an extended family network where parents, siblings, and other kin (real and fictive) help in the adjustment to the role of parent (Furstenberg & Crawford, 1978; Stack, 1974). Even though friends were among a group of possible sources of support in the category identified as "other," it was unlikely that African American adolescents considered it the most appropriate option since friends are often considered to be "family."

Results of these analyses for White teenagers, as a group, were also consistent with studies of social support with predominately White samples. Poor, unmarried White teenagers were found to expect the support of male partners more frequently than any other source for labor and delivery and child care and to expect that their families would assist them with chores. An explanation for the latter finding has already been put forth. An interpretation of the former is offered by Thompson (1986), who contends that conflicts between traditional values in White families and the increasing proportion of White teens becoming pregnant and opting to parent may force these mothers to live outside their culture, thereby lacking appropriate support. Wandersman et al. (1980) contend that husbands and boyfriends usually serve as primary source of support for White mothers during the early stages of motherhood. As the child grows, there is a tendency to rely more on the support of one's family.

Interest in Pregnancy vs. Interest in the Child

Level of husband/boyfriend interest in pregnancy was compared with the amount of interest shown in the child during the first two years of life. Results indicate that poor, unmarried African American adolescents assigned to the nurse-visited group were more likely to report greater male partner interest in their pregnancies at intake but not at 8 months of pregnancy. Olds et al. (1988) also reported the former finding among poor, unmarried mothers in the general PEIP sample population. Moreover, women in this group experienced increased levels of interest in their children over time. The difference between nurse-visited and control group teenagers was significant when children were 6 months of age (p<.001). Ninety-seven percent of all poor, unmarried adolescents in the nurse-visited group reported a lot of interest in their child on the part of their husband or boyfriend. Among African American and White adolescents alike, the proportion of women in the nurse-visited group reporting male partners with a lot of interest in their children was highly significant at 6 months (p<.01) and at 22 months (p<.01). This was also true for African American adolescent mothers when their children were 10 and 22 months of age (both being significant at p<.05). These findings suggest a positive impact of home visitation on husband/boyfriend interest in the pregnancies and children of African American adolescent mothers.

Increased interest in children did not, unfortunately, translate into additional help with child care or chore support. While level of interest was found to be significant for all nurse-visited groups, with over time effects for African American mothers in particular, no significant main effects were found for other types of support. Trends toward increased child care and chore support, however, were noticed during the early assessment periods, as reflected in the following discussion.

SUPPORT PERSON BEHAVIOR AND CHILD CARE AND CHORES SUPPORT

Observations of support person behavior with the newborns, conducted by hospital maternity nurses, were compared with reports of support received for child care responsibilities and household chores. Ratings were found to favor poor, unmarried White teenagers, irrespective of treatment group assignment. Support persons for White adolescents assigned nurse-visits were much more likely than were the supports of control group mothers to have their interactions with newborns rated positively by maternity nurses. Between 14% and 19% of supports for the former group were observed in positive interactions compared to only 9%-12.5% of control group support persons.

Discussion

The lack of positive ratings among African American support persons may be explained by the initial disapproval that many African American adolescents confront before giving birth to their infants. Thompson (1986) indicates that in spite of initial parental disapproval and rejection about pregnancy, African American adolescent mothers experience a marshaling of support from the extended family system. It is feasible that adolescents in this group did not have supportive others with them during the labor and delivery process as a result of disapproval. The data reflect the trend to which Thompson refers, with increased support among African American adolescent mothers after the birth of their child.

Results suggest that maternity nurse observations were a good predictor of support with child care responsibilities but not of support for chores among poor, unmarried White mothers in the nurse-visited treatment group. Mothers assigned home-visitation were much more likely than were controls to receive support with child care responsibilities at 6 and 22 months. This finding suggests that nurses were able to improve the amount of support adolescent mothers received once their children were born.

Contrary to the above finding were more frequent reports for chore support among poor, unmarried White and African American teenagers in the control group. Women in the control groups received more support for household chores than their nurse-visited counterparts over time. The previous explanation, while logical, necessarily makes it difficult to hypothesize about the following results. Data indicated that African American adolescents in the control group were significantly more likely to have been receiving support with child care responsibilities at 6 months ($p<.05$) and assistance with chores at both 6 ($p<.05$) and 22 months ($p<.10$) than mothers in the nurse-visited group. Results of regression analyses showed an effect for chore support at intake ($p<.03$) and for support with chores at 6 months ($p<.001$) in predicting the respective support outcomes. An interaction effect for treatment x race was also found when predicting support for chores at 22 months ($p<.10$). The interaction indicated that African American mothers in the control group were significantly more likely than White mothers in the same group to report support for domestic chores at the 22 month assessment.

In the previous explanation, the argument was that teenage mothers may have simply underestimated their resources. The same may well apply in this case. It may also be the case that a number of potential supports for nurse-visited adolescents distance themselves from the young mother and her newborn, under the assumption that the nurse-visits are formal and geared more toward immediate support network members like family members and male partners. Since these group were the primary focus of nurses, it is possible that that message may have been conveyed in some way to other, more distant support network members (e.g., friends or relatives). A more appropriate explanation for this finding cannot be offered, as there are no data in the literature that speaks to it.

EXPLANATION OF LACK OF EFFECTS OF THE PEIP

As indicated earlier in the discussion of methodological problems that have contributed to conflicting results reported in early intervention studies, there are a number of possible explanations for the lack of evidence in support of the PEIP. The two that are perhaps most relevant to the present study have to do with measurement and sample size. Halpern (1984) suggests that variations in outcome measures make it difficult to have confidence in and interpret results of intervention studies.

Although the PEIP included a component which sought to enhance the informal networks of socially disadvantaged families, social support was not measured as an outcome variable. A number of comprehensive programs have been developed for families at-risk for social, health, and economic problems. However, there are relatively few which include social support as key components. For those that do, rarely is the construct used as an outcome measure of program effectiveness. The present study was conducted to determine the role of social support in improving the lives of at-risk adolescent mothers and their children by trying to understand the impact of a comprehensive early intervention program on the availability of social support to young mothers.

In addition to striving to address yet unanswered questions regarding the role of social support in the lives of African American and White adolescent mothers, the present study was also hindered by the relatively small African American sample employed. It is well documented that small sample sizes decrease the sensitivity of evaluation designs to the possible occurrence of effects. As reflected in Olds et al.'s (1986) unpublished manuscript and stated in various publications of results from the White sample, it is difficult to find

Discussion

statistically significant results since the statistical procedures needed to model complex interactions can often not be done. Halpern (1984) confirms this by stating that the most powerful effects of a program will likely be masked by a small sample.

In light of these and others limitations discussed in Chapter 3, it is not surprising that more solid evidence for the PEIP was not found. It is, however, important to note that the findings reported here do suggest that the program is effective in some instances, even if not statistically significant in all cases. The results show interesting differences in the support networks of poor, unmarried African American and White adolescent mothers, as well as the different ways in which these networks are impacted by participation in an early intervention program. In this way, the present study adds considerably to the body of literature that seeks to investigate the role of social support within the context of intervention programs. The implications for policy are discussed in the following chapter.

CHAPTER 6
Policy Implications and Conclusion

As noted earlier, the PEIP has been influential in renewing the interest of policy-makers services at both the state and national levels. Recommendations for increased funding for such services have been put forth based on the contention that home-based support for families may counteract health, educational, and developmental problems confronted by our nation's most disadvantaged children and families. Results of the present study, however, raise at least two important questions: 1) Should government officials provide more, less, or continued levels of funding for support interventions; and 2) Are home visitation interventions the appropriate type of interventions to employ? Or, are there other types of early intervention strategies which may be more effective? Each of these questions will be addressed in turn. Additionally, I will discuss the implications of this work for future research with ethnically diverse samples.

Given what has been learned from this secondary analysis of the PEIP data, arguments for future levels of funding could easily go in any of the three above-stated directions. Arguments for increased funding, based on these data, would be necessarily difficult in light of the present political climate. There is, however, a basis on which an argument for continued funding could be made. Consider the following: It is well documented that teenage fathers are largely absent from the lives of their children. The proportion of out-of-wedlock births among adolescent mothers is quite high (estimates range from 65%-80%), with the rate among Black teenagers reaching astronomical proportions (estimates are above 90%).

While evidence in support of the PEIP did not show increased assistance with child care and chores, it indicated that the levels of interest in children on the part of husbands and boyfriends was enhanced as a result of the intervention. Phrased in a slightly different way, data did not suggest that being exposed to home visitation enhanced male partner interest in such a way as to have it translate into support with child care responsibilities and household tasks. This notwithstanding, the importance of increased interest in children on the part of husbands and boyfriends cannot be underestimated. The implications for this are great, especially if one takes into account current political debate regarding family structure and values and the enforcement of child support laws.

Without question a first step to preserving family structure and increasing family values would be to somehow draw into the lives of women and children what would otherwise be absent fathers. The data here indicate that nurse visitation services were successful in getting adolescent fathers to take an active interest in their children. That was a major accomplishment, particularly among Black adolescents where the absence of young fathers is most visible. Enforcement of child support laws would become considerably easier if such services continued to generate high levels of interest on the part of biological fathers.

With proposed cuts to cash benefit programs like Aid to Families with Dependent Children (AFDC) in an attempt to reform the welfare system as we know it, support interventions seem an important way of helping families transition to self-sufficiency. A reallocation of resources to fund support interventions that enhance the natural support systems of disadvantaged families would, over time, relieve the government of the continued burden of supporting families. The value of support interventions using nurse home visits lies in the ability of such programs to improve the informal support networks of families. To the extent that home visitation remains grounded within communities, the possibilities for success are great.

Nurse home visits are an ideal approach to assisting families since many historically underserved populations, like that of the Black community, exist within the confines of extended networks. It is my contention that more thought needs to be given to involving respective communities in the intervention process. That is, if home visitation programs were committed to drawing upon well-respected community members to act as home visitors, the likelihood of success with some groups would increase substantially. Often times, researchers employ members of such communities who meet a certain educational criteria

Policy Implications and Conclusion

but who are not as nested in their communities as some other members. Who to recruit and train is crucial, and I would be inclined to think that long-standing members of communities tend to hold the most hope for reaching skeptical, reluctant, or isolated families. Trust is a major issue, particularly in the Black community. The process of trust-building would be considerably enhanced if identifiable members of targeted communities were involved in the intervention strategy.

Communities are frequently not asked their perceptions about problems in their neighborhoods. When invited to engage in discussions about problem identification and resolution, communities probably have a wealth of insight about the most appropriate strategies for reaching their members. I think nurse-visiting programs could be enhanced by incorporating the voices of communities. To do so, it seems, would increase the likelihood of success since communities know best what their needs are (even if they cannot always articulate them well) and how to most effectively reach their members.

A universal approach to resolving problems tends to be used far too frequently. A prime example of this is again the Black community. In the present study, it was found that Black adolescents benefited most from the PEIP with regard to enhanced male partner interest in their infants. It seems that the program, which was comprised of a predominantly White sample, was not particularly tailored to the needs of Black adolescent mothers. For example, the way in which interest was defined for the sample population may not have been consistent with the way in which Black women think about or interpret interest. Often times, in the Black community, interest is defined by actions as simple as providing pampers or other tangible items for the child, having paternal family members involved in the child's life, or calls from the male partner regarding the child's well-being. Rarely would interest in the child be defined solely by direct contact or interaction. Increased interest in children represents a big step forward, but it may have been the case that involving young males at that level was the maximum achievable goal for this program given how goals were defined.

Contrary to the hypothesis, Black control group mothers received more support with chores and child care. The lack of evidence for this type of support among nurse-visited adolescents may very much be related to how those tasks were defined. If women in this group expected that their support persons should have behaved in a certain way, failure to meet that expectation would have necessarily resulted in low levels of reported support. Conversely, support persons may have been under the assumption that adolescents' involvement in the intervention either precluded their involvement or demanded more of them than they could deliver. In either case—that is, whether expectations were assigned to nurses by women and their support members or were, in fact, real—support would have been hindered. Control group mothers, who were not exposed to nurses were presumably able to operate more freely from their own definitions of support.

To the extent that early interventions services are tailored to the needs of specific communities, the data here suggest that there is hope for continued improvements in the lives of children and their families. Nurse-visiting operates on the principle that serving the needs of families in their own communities is key to improving the health and development of children. Incorporating communities into the development and implementation stages of such interventions is crucial if we are to gain a sound understanding of communities' needs for problem resolution. Discontinuing the pattern of applying all programs to all sample populations would be greatly enhanced if community voices are brought to bear on any or all intervention strategies. Certainly, home visitation offers a wealth of potential information about how to help families support themselves relying largely on their informal support networks. Keeping families nested in communities and enabling community members to sustain families provides hope for a brighter tomorrow for all concerned.

According to Zigler & Black (1989), more research is needed to affect policy and result in family and community-based initiatives that enable practitioners to work with families in their current forms; that provide support that help alleviate the specific stressors confronting them; and that encourage families to find ways to promote their own health and well-being. In the interim, I think the case for continued support for home visitation-based interventions is strengthened by the data presented herein.

Bibliography

Achenbach, T.M., Phares, V., Howell, C.T., Rauh, V.A., & Nurcombe, B. 1990. Seven-year outcome of the Vermont intervention program for low birth weight infants. *Child Development*, 61(6):1672-1681.

Badger, E., Burns, D., & Rhoads, B. 1976. Education for adolescent mothers in a hospital setting. *American Journal of Public Health*, 66(5):469-472.

Bailey, D.B., & Simeonsson, R.J. "Family assessment in early intervention." Columbus, OH: Merrill Publishing Company, 1988.

Baldwin, W., & Cain, V.S. 1980. The children of teenage parents. *Family Planning Perspectives*, 12(1):34-43.

Barnett, A.P. Sociocultural influences on adolescent mothers. In R. Staples (Ed.), "The Black family: Essays and Studies." Belmont, CA: Wadsworth Publishing Co., 1991.

Barrera, M., Jr. Social support in the adjustment of pregnant adolescents: Assessment issues. In B.H. Gottlieb (Ed.), "Social networks and social support strategies." Beverly Hills, CA: Sage Publications, 1981.

Barth, R.P. 1988. Social skill and social support among young mothers. *Journal of Community Psychology*, 16(2):132-143.

Barth, R.P., Schinke, S.P., & Maxwell, J.S. 1983. Psychological correlates of teenage motherhood. *Journal of Youth and Adolescence*, 12(6):471-487.

Brooks-Gunn, J., & Chase-Lansdale, P.L. 1991. Adolescent childbearing: Effects on children. *Encyclopedia of Adolescence*, 1:103-106.

Bronfenbrenner, U. Is early intervention effective? In M. Guttentag and E.L. Struening (Eds) "Handbook of evaluation research" (pp. 519-604). Beverly Hills: Sage Publications, 1975.

Bronfenbrenner, U. "Is early intervention effective?" Washington, DC: US Department of Health, Education, and Welfare. Office of Child Development, 1974.

Bryant, D.M., & Ramey, G.T. An analysis of the effectiveness of early intervention programs for environmentally at-risk children. In M.J. Guralnick & F.C. Bennett (Eds.), "The effectiveness of early intervention for at-risk and handicapped children" (pp. 33-78). Orlando, Florida: Academic Press, Inc., 1987.

Campbell, T.L. 1994. Impact of prenatal/early infancy home visitation on family health. *Family Systems Medicine*, 12(1):81-85.

Coates, D.L., & Van Widenfelt, B. 1991. Pregnancy in adolescence. *Encyclopedia of Adolescence*, 2:794-782.

Cochran, M., & Bassard, J. 1979. Child development and personal social networks. *Child Development, 50(3)*:601-616.

Cochran, M., Larner, M., Riley, D., Gunnarsson, L., & Henderson, C.H., Jr. (Eds.). " Extending families: The social networks of parents and their children. " Cambridge, MA: Cambridge University Press, 1990.

Cohen, S., & Syme, L.S. (Eds.). "Social support and health." Orlando, FL: Academic Press, Inc., 1985.

Colletta, N.D. 1981. Social support and the risk of maternal rejection by adolescent mothers. *Journal of Psychology*, 109(2):191-197.

Colletta, N.D., & Lee, D. 1983. The impact of support for Black adolescent mothers. *Journal of Family Issues*, 4(1):127-143.

Cooley, M.L. & Unger, D.G. 1991. The role of family support in determining developmental outcomes in children of teen mothers. *Child Psychiatry and Human Development*, 21(3):217-234.

Crnic, K.A., Greenberg, M.T., Ragozin, A.S., Robinson, N.M., & Basham, R.B. 1983. Effects of stress and social support on mothers and premature and full-term infants. *Child Development*, 54(1):209-217.

Crnic, K.A., Greenberg, M.T., Robinson, N.M., & Ragozin, A.S. 1984. Maternal stress and social support: Effects on the mother-infant relationship from birth to eighteen months. *American Journal of Orthopsychiatry*, 54(2):224-235.

Crockenberg, S. 1981. Infant irritability, mother responsiveness, and social support influences on the security of infant-mother attachment. *Child Development*, 52(3):857-865.

Crockenberg, S. 1987. Predictors and correlates of anger toward and punitive control of toddlers by adolescent mothers. *Child Development*, 58(4):964-975.

Cutrona, C.E. 1984. Social support and stress in the transition to parenthood. *Journal of Abnormal Psychology*, 93(4):378-390.

Davis, R. 1988. Adolescent pregnancy and infant mortality: Isolating the effects of race. *Adolescence,* 23(92):899-908.

Bibliography

Dawson, P., Robinson, J.L., & Johnson, C.B. 1982. Informal social support as an intervention. *Zero to Three*, 3(2):1-5.

Dawson, P., Van Doorninck, W.J., & Robinson, J.L. 1989. Effects of home-based, informal social support on child health. *Developmental and Behavioral Pediatrics*, 10(2):63-68.

de Anda, D. & Becerra, R.M. 1984. Support networks for adolescent mothers. *Social Casework: The Journal of Contemporary Social Work*, 65(3):172-181.

de Lissovoy, V. 1973. Child care by adolescent parents. *Children Today*, 2(4):22-25.

Dimitrovsky, L., Perez-Hirshberg, M., & Itskowitz, R. 1986. Depression during and following pregnancy: Quality of family relationships. *Journal of Psychology*, 121(3):213-218.

Dore, M.M., & Dumois, A.O. 1990. Cultural differences in the meaning of adolescent pregnancy. *Families in Society*, 71(2), 93-101.

Dunst, C.J., Vance, S.D., & Cooper, C.S. 1986. A social systems perspective of adolescent pregnancy: Determinants of parent and parent-child behavior. *Infant Mental Health Journal*, 7(1):34-48.

Eckenrode, J. 1983. The mobilization of social supports: Some individual constraints. *American Journal of Psychology*, 11(5):509-528.

Eckenrode, J., & Gore, S. Stressful events and social supports: The significance of context. In B.H. Gottlieb (Ed.), "Social networks and social strategies." Beverly Hills, CA: Sage Publications, 1981.

Eckenrode, J., & Wethington, E. The process and outcome of mobilized social support. In S. Duck and R. C. Silver (Eds.), "Personal relationships and social support " (pp. 83-103). London, England: Sage Publications, 1990.

Field, T., Widmayer, S., Adler, S., & DeCubas, M. 1990. Teenage parenting in different cultures, family constellations, and care giving environments: Effects on infant development. *Infant Mental Health Journal*, 11(2):158-174.

Field, T., Widmayer, S., Greenberg, R., & Stoller, S. 1982. Effects of parent training on teenage mothers and their infants. *Pediatrics*, 69(6):703-707.

Field, T., Widmayer, S., Stringer, S., & Ignatoff, E. 1980. Teenage, lower-class, Black mothers and their pre-term infants: An intervention and developmental follow-up. *Child Development*, 51(2):426-436.

Furstenberg, F.F., Jr. "Unplanned parenthood: The social consequences of teenage childbearing." New York: Free Press, 1976.

Furstenberg, F.F., Jr., & Crawford, A.G. 1978. Family support: Helping teenage mothers to cope. *Family Planning Perspectives*, 10(6):322-333.

Garbarino, J. Social support networks: RX for the helping professionals. In J. K. Whittaker, J.K., & J. Garbarino (Eds.). "Social support networks: Informal helping in the human services" (pp. 3-28). New York: Aldine Publishing Company, 1983.

Garcia-Coll, C.T., Hoffman, J., Van Houten, L.J., & Oh, W. 1987. The social context of teenage childbearing: Effects on the infant's care-giving environment. *Journal of Youth and Adolescence*, 16(4):345-360.

Geronimus, A.T. 1987. On teenage childbearing and neonatal mortality in the United States. *Population and Development Review*, 13(2):245-279.

Gottlieb, B.H. (Ed.). Social networks and social support strategies. Beverly Hills: Sage Publications, 1981.

Gottlieb, B.H. (Ed.). "Social support strategies: Guidelines for mental health practice." Beverly Hills: Sage Publications, 1983.

Gottlieb, B.H. (Ed.). "Marshaling social support: Format, processes, and effects." Beverly Hills: Sage Publications, 1988.

Gottlieb, B.H., & Wagner, F. Stress and support processes in close relationships. In J. Eckenrode (Ed.), "The social context of coping" (pp. 165-188). New York: Plenum Press, 1991.

Gray, S.W., & Ramey, B.K. 1986. Adolescent childbearing and high school completion. *Journal of Applied Developmental Psychology*, 7(3):167-179.

Gray, S.W., & Wandersman, L.P. 1980. The methodology of home-based intervention studies: Problems and promising strategies. *Child Development*, 51(4):993-1009.

Gutelius, M.F., Kirsch, A.D., MacDonald, S., Brooks, M.R., & McErlean, T. 1977. Controlled study of child health supervision: Behavioral results. *Pediatrics*, 60(3):294-303.

Halpern, R. 1984. Lack of effects for home-based early intervention? Some possible explanations. *American Journal of Orthopsychiatry*, 54(1):33-42.

House, J.S., & Kahn, R.L. Measures and concepts of social support. In S. Cohen and L.S. Syme (Eds.), "Social support and health" (pp. 83-108). Orlando, FL: Academic Press, Inc., 1985.

Hutchins, V.L., & McPherson, M. 1991. National Agenda for children with special health needs: Social policy for the 1990s through the 21st century. *American Psychologist*, 46(2):141-143.

Jones, F.A., Green, V., & Krauss, D.R. 1980. Maternal responsiveness of primiparous mothers during the postpartum period: Age differences. *Pediatrics*, 65(3):579-583.

Kang, R., Barnard, K., Hammond, M., Oshio, S., et al. 1994. Pre-term infant follow-up project: A multi-site field experiment of hospital and home intervention programs for mothers and pre-term infants. *Public Health Nursing*, 12(3):171-180.

Klein, H.A., & Cordell, A.S. 1987. The adolescent as mother: Early risk identification. *Journal of Youth and Adolescence*, 16(1):47-58.

Kissman, K. 1988. Factors associated with competence, well-being, and parenting attitudes among teen mothers. *International Journal of Adolescence and Youth*, 1(3):247-255.

Kissman, K., & Shapiro, J. 1990. The composites of social support and well-being among adolescent mothers. *International Journal of Adolescence and Youth*, 2(3):165-173.

Koniak-Griffin, D., & Verzemnieks, I. 1991. Effects of nursing intervention on adolescents' maternal role attainment. *Issues in Comprehensive Pediatric Nursing*, 14:121-138.

Lally, J.R., Mangione, P.L., & Honig, A.S. 1988. The Syracuse University family development research program: Lone-range impact on an early intervention with low-income children and their families. In R.D. Powell (Ed.), Parent education as early childhood intervention: Emerging directions in theory, research, and practice (pp. 79-104). *Advances in Applied Developmental Psychology*, 3.

Landy, S., Schubert, J., Cleland, & Montgomery, J.S. 1984. The effect of research with teenage mothers on the development of their infants. *Journal of Applied Social Psychology*, 14(5):461-468.

Lazar, I., & Darlington, R. 1982. Lasting effects of early education: A report from the consortium for Longitudinal Studies. *Monographs of the Society for Research in child Development*, 47, (2-3, Serial No. 195).

Levine, L., Garcia-Coll, C.T., & Oh, W. 1985. Determinants of mother-infant interaction in adolescent mothers. *Pediatrics*, 75(1):23-29.

Madden, J., O'Hara, J., & Levenstein, P. 1984. Home Again: Effects of the mother-child home program on mother and child. *Child Development*, 55(2):636-647.

Manns, W. Support systems of significant others in Black families. In H.P. McAdoo (Ed.), "Black families." Beverly Hills: Sage Publications, 1981.

Marcenko, M.G., & Spence, M. 1994. Home visitation services for at-risk pregnant and postpartum women: A randomized trial. *American Journal of Orthopsychiatry*, 64 (3):468-478.

Mayfield-Brown, L. 1989. Family status of low-income adolescent mothers. *Journal of Adolescent Research*, 4(2):202-213.

McAnarney, E.R., Lawrence, R.A., Ricciuti, H.N., Polley, J., & Szilgyi, M. 1986. Interactions of adolescent mothers and their 1-year-old children. *Pediatrics*, 78(4):585-590.

McDonough, S.C. 1984. Intervention programs for adolescent mothers and their offspring. *Journal of Chidren in Contemprary Society*, 17(1):67-78.

McHenry, P.C., Walters, L.H., & Johnson, C. 1979. Adolescent pregnancy: A review of the literature. *The Family Coordinator*, 18:17-28.

Miller, S. The adolescent parents project: Sharing the transition. In M. Larner, R. Halpern, & O. Harkavy (Eds.), "Fair start for children: Lessons learned from seven demonstration projects " (pp.15-134). New Haven, CT: Yale University Press, 1992.

Moran, M.A. 1985. Families in early intervention: Effects of program variables. *Zero to Three*, 5(5):11-14.

Nagy, M. C., Leeper, J.D., Hullett-Robertson, S., & Northrup, R.S. The rural Alabama pregnancy and infant health project: A rural clinic reaches out. In M. Larner, R. Halpern, & O. Harkavy (Eds.), "Fair start for children: Lessons learned from seven demonstration projects" (pp. 91-114). New Haven, CT: Yale University Press, 1992.

National Commission to Prevent Infant Mortality. "Death before life: The tragedy of infant mortality." Washington, D.C., 1988.

National Commission to Prevent Infant Mortality. "Home visiting: Opening doors for America's pregnant women and children." Washington, D.C., 1989.

Olds, D.L. Can home visitation improve the health of women and children at environmental risk? In D.E. Rogers & E. Ginzberg (Eds.), "Improving the life chances of children at risk." Westview press: Boulder, CO., 1990.

Olds, D.L. 1984. Case studies of factors interfering with nurse home visitors' promotion of positive care-giving methods in high risk families. *Early Child Development and Care*, 16(1-2):149-166.

Olds, D.L., Eckenrode, J., Henderson, C.R., Kitzman, H., Powers, J., et al. 1997. Long-term effects of home visitation on maternal life course and child abuse and neglect: Fifteen-year follow-up of a randomized trial. *Journal of the American Medical Association*, 278(8):637-643.

Olds, D.L., Henderson, C.R., Birmingham, M.T., Chamberlin, R., & Tatelbaum, R. "Final Report: Prenatal/Early Infancy Project." Rockville, MD: Bureau of Community health Services, HSA, PHS, DHHS, 1983.

Olds, D.L., Henderson, C.R., Chamberlin, R., & Tatelbaum, R. 1988. Improving the life-course development of socially disadvantaged mothers: A randomized trial of nurse home visitation. *American Journal of Public Health*, 78(11):1436-1445.

Bibliography

Olds, D.L., Henderson, C.R., Chamberlin, R., & Tatelbaum, R. "Prenatal/early infancy project: Impact on minority women and children." Unpublished manuscript, 1986.

Olds, D.L., & Kitzman, H. 1990. Can home visitation improve the health of women and children at environmental risk? *Pediatrics*, 86(1):108-116.

Panzarine, S. 1988. Teen mothering: Behaviors and interventions. *Journal of Adolescent Health Care*, 9(5):443-448.

Pearlin, L.I. Social structure and processes of social. In S. Cohen and L.S. Syme (Eds.), *"Social support and health"* (pp. 43-60). Orlando, FL: Academic Press, Inc., 1985.

Phipps-Yonas, S. 1980. Teenage pregnancy and motherhood. *American Journal of Orthopsychiatry*, 50(3):403-431.

Pilisuk, M., & Hillier-Parks, S. 1980. Structural dimensions of social support groups. *The Journal of Psychology*, 106:157-177.

Powell, D.R. 1980. Personal social networks as a focus for primary prevention of child mistreatment. *Infant Mental Health Journal*, 1(4):232-239.

Ragozin, A.S., Basham, R.B., Crnic, K.A., Greenberg, M.T., & Robinson, N.M. 1982. Effects of maternal age on parenting role. *Developmental Psychology*, 18(4):627-634.

Ramey, C.T., & Suarez, T.M. 1984. Early intervention and the early experience paradigm: Toward a better framework for social policy. *Journal of Children in Contemporary Society*, 17(1):3-13.

Rhodes, J.E., Ebert, L., & Fischer, K. 1992. Natural mentors: An overlooked resource in the social networks of young, African-American mothers. *American Journal of Community Psychology*, 20(4):445-461.

Rhodes, J.E., & Woods, M. 1995. Comfort and conflict in the relationships of pregnant, minority adolescents: Social support as a moderator of social strain. *Journal of Community Psychology*, 23(1):74-84.

Richardson, R.A., Barbara, N.B., & Bubenzer, D.L. 1991. Bittersweet connections: Informal networks as sources of support and interference for adolescent mothers. *Family Relations*, 40(4):430-434.

Riley, D., & Eckenrode, J. 1986. Social ties: Subgroup differences in costs and benefits. *Journal of Personality and Social Psychology*, 51(4):770-778.

Roberts, R.N., Wasik, B.H., Casto, G., & Ramey, C.T. 1991. Family support in the home: Program, policy, and social change. *American Psychologist*, 42(2):131-137.

Roosa, M.W., Fitzgerald, H.E., & Carlson, N.A. 1982a. A comparison of teenage and older mothers: A systems analysis. *Journal of Marriage and the Family*, 44(2):367-377.

Roosa, M.W., Fitzgerald, H.E., & Carlson, N.A. 1982b. Teenage and older mothers and their infants: A descriptive comparison. *Adolescence*, 17(65):1-17.

Rosenbaum, S., Layton, C., & Liu, J. "The health of America's children." Washington, DC: The Children's Defense Fund, 1991.

Schilmoeller, G.L., Baranowski, M.D., & Higgins, B.S. 1991. Long-term support and personal adjustment of adolescent and older mothers. *Adolescence*, 26(104):787-797.

Schinke, S. P. 1978. Teenage pregnancy: The need for multiple casework services. *Social Casework*, 59(7):406-410.

Seitz, V., Rosenbaum, L.K., & Apfel, N.H. 1985. Effects of family support intervention: A ten-year follow-up. *Child Development*, 56(2):376-391.

Seymore, C., Frothingham, T.E., MacMillan, J., & Durant, R.H. 1990. Child development knowledge, child rearing attitudes, and social support among first- and second-time mothers. *Journal of Adolescent Health Care*, 11(4):343-350.

Siegel, E., Bauman, K.E., Schaefer, E.S., Saunders, M.M., & Ingram, D.D. 1980. Hospital and home support during infancy: Impact on maternal attachment, child abuse and neglect, and health care utilization. *Pediatrics*, 66(2):183-190.

Slaughter, D.T. 1983. Early intervention and its effects on maternal and child development. *Monographs of the Society for Research in Child Development*, 48(4), (Serial No. 202).

Stack, C.B. "All our kin: Strategies for survival in a Black community." New York: Harper and Row Publishers, 1974.

Stevens, J.H., Jr. 1988. Social support, locus of control, and parenting in three low-income groups of mothers: Black teenagers, Black adults, and White adults. *Child Development*, 59(3):635-642.

Stiffman, A.R. 1991. Adolescent mothers: Racial differences in child rearing support. Child and Adolescent Social Work, 8(5):369-386.

Stone, W.L., Bendell, C. & Field, T.M. 1988. The impact of socioeconomic status on teenage mothers and children who received early intervention. *Journal of Applied Developmental Psychology*, 9(4):391-408.

Thompson, M.S. "The influence of supportive relations on the psychological well-being of teenage mothers." Raleigh, NC: University of North Carolina Press, 1986.

Thompson, R.J., Cappleman, M.W., Conrad, H.H., & Jordan, W.B. 1982. Early intervention program for adolescent mothers and their infants. *Developmental and Behavioral Pediatrics*, 3(1):18-21.

Teti, D.M., & Gelfand, D.M. 1991. Behavioral competence among mothers of infants in the first year: The mediational role of maternal self-efficacy. *Child Development*, 62(5):918-929.

Tracy, E.M., & Whittaker, J.K. 1987. The evidence base for social support interventions in child and family practice: Emerging issues for research and practice. *Children and Youth Services Review*, 9(4):249-270.

Turner, R.J., Grindstaff, C.F., and Phillips, N. 1990. Social support and outcome in teenage pregnancy. *Journal of Health and Social Behavior*, 31(1):43-57.

Unger, D.G., & Wandersman, L.P. 1985. Social support and adolescent mothers: Action research contributions to theory and application. *Journal of Social Issues*, 41(1):29-45.

Unger, D.G., & Wandersman, L.P. 1988. The relation of family and partner support to the adjustment of adolescent mothers. *Child Development*, 59(4):1056-1060.

Upchurch, D.M., & McCarthy, J. 1990. The timing of a first birth and high school completion. *American Sociological Review*, 55(2):224-234.

US Congress, Office of Technology Assessment. "Health children: Investing in the future." OTA-H-345. Washington, D.C.: US Government Printing Office, 1988.

Wandersman, L., Wandersman, A., & Kahn, S. 1980. Social support in the transition to parenthood. *Journal of Community Psychology*, 8:332-342.

Ware, L.M., Osofsky, J.D., Eberhart-Wright, A., & Leichtman, M.L. 1987. Challenges of home visitor interventions with adolescent mothers and their infants. *Infant Mental Health Journal*, 8(4):418-428.

Wasserman, G.A., Rauh, V.A., Brunelli, S.A., Garcia-Castro, M., & Necos, B. 1990a. Psychological attributes and life experiences of disadvantaged minority mothers: Age and ethnic variations. *Child Development*, 61(2):566-580.

Wasserman, G.A., Brunelli, S.A., & Rauh, V.A. 1990b. Social supports and living arrangements of adolescent and adult mothers. *Journal of Adolescent Research*, 5(1):54-67.

Wasik, B.H., Ramey, C.T., Bryant, D.M., & Sparling, J.J. 1990. A longitudinal study of two early intervention strategies: Project CARE. *Child Development*, 61(6):1682-1696.

Weiss, H.B. Family support and education programs: Working through ecological theories of human development. In H.B. Weiss and F.H. Jacobs. "Evaluating family programs" (pp. 3-36). New York: Aldine De Gruyter Publishers, 1988.

Weissbourd, B., & Kagan, S. L. 1989. Family support programs: Catalysts for change. *American Journal of Orthopsychiatry*, 59(1):20-31.

Whitman, T.L., Borkowski, J.G., Schellenbach, T. & Nath, P.S. 1987. Predicting and understanding developmental delay of children of adolescent mothers: A multidimensional approach. *American Journal of Mental Deficiency*, 92(1):40-56.

Whittaker, J.K., & Garbarino, J. (Eds.). "Social support networks: Informal helping in the human services." New York: Aldine Publishing Company, 1983.

Zigler, E., & Black, K. B. (1989). America's family support movement: Strengths and litmitations. *American Journal of Orthopsychiatry*, 59(1):6-19.

Zuckerman, B., Winsmore, G., & Alpert, J.J. 1979. A study of attitudes and support systems in inner-city adolescent mothers. *Adolescent Medicine*, 95(1):122-125.

Index

Anticipated vs. actual support
   Treatment group
      differences, 62
Adolescence
   operationalized, 53
Adolescent childbearing, 3-4
Adolescent Parenting
   Adjustment to mothering
      role, 82
Analysis
   Cross-tabulations, 56
   Descriptive statistics, 56
   multiple regression, 56
Anticipated support, 60
   Child care, 60
   With chores, 60-61
Anticipated Vs Actual Support
   for labor/delivery, 62
   Treatment group
      differences, 62-63
   Race Differences, 63
At-risk children, 7

Birth rate. *See* Fertility rate
Buffering effect, 5, 17

Child maltreatment, 3, 39, 42

Child outcomes. *See*
   Developmental outcomes
Child rearing. *See* Parenting
   practices
Chi-square statistic
   Pearson, 56
Community, 6
Control variables, 59
Cross tabulations
   testing bi-variate
      relationships. *See*
      Analysis
Depression, 4, 22-24, 42
Developmental delay, 4, 32, 39
Developmental outcomes, 4,
   24
   Influence of early
      intervention on, 32

Early intervention, 6, 10, 36
   as a prevention strategy, 31-
   33
Early intervention programs
   effectiveness of, 34
   impact on cognitive
      development, 34-38

impact on maternal and
child outcomes, 38-41
impact on parent-child
interaction, 41-43
for adolescent mothers, 43
Economically disadvantaged
families, 6
employment
securing, 4, 20, 38
unemployment
under-employment, 3

Fertility rate
Adolescent fertility, 3, 5
Findings
Summary of, 76

Home visiting
nurse visits, 7, 8, 36, 39,
40- 41
Human service programs, 6, 8,
9, 38

Infant development, 8, 46
Infant mortality, 3, 4
Informal Support, 5, 8, 9, 14,
26, 28, 39, 40
Internal locus of control, 4, 24,
35
Interpersonal relationships, 5-
6, 14
Interpersonal support
social networks, 5, 14
Interventions
family interventions, 9
family support, 6-7

Kinship ties, 5

Limitations of the Data, 57

Long-term consequences, 4

Male partner interest, 67
in pregnancy, 67
in their children, 67
Race differences, 69-70
Treatment group
differences, 67-68
Maternal functioning. *See*
Parenting attitudes and
Parental behaviors
Methodological problems, 6,
11, 32
definition, 6, 32
Moderating effect of race, 81
on labor/delivery, child
care, and chore support,
86-88
on male partner interest, 89-
90
on source of support at
intake, 88-89
Mothering role, 4, 13

Out-of-wedlock pregnancy, 3-
4

Paradigm, 6, 9
Parental attitudes, 4
Parental behaviors, 4, 8-10, 17,
26, 35, 39, 41, 45, 48, 55
influence of early
intervention on, 32
Parenting
adjustment to, 19
attitudes, 13
behaviors, 13
demands of, 20
practices, 4, 19
Parenting practices, 24, 28, 40

Index

Policy implications, 95-98
Policy-makers, 3, 5, 6, 8, 10
Practitioners, 6, 8, 10
Prenatal care, 4, 19, 39, 41
Prenatal/Early Infancy Project
  description of the, 7, 51-52
Primary prevention, 6

Racial differences in social
  support
  among adolescents, 29
Regression analysis
  Step-wise linear. *See*
  Analysis

Sample size, 53
Sampe and procedure, 53-54
Secondary analysis
  of data, 51
  Single parenthood, 7
Social context, 4, 6, 19, 22, 24
  of adolescent pregnancy
  and parenting, 20-24
Social support, 5, 9, 10, 14-15,
  21-26, 35, 40, 89, 92
  Among older vs. younger
  adolescents, 22
  As a component of early
  interventions, 6
  Availability and utilization,
  24-28
  Concept of, 5-6
  Definition of, 5
  Effect on maternal and
  child health, 6
  Extended family as, 20
  Functional/instrumental, 55
  Health-promoting effects
  of, 8, 13
  Impact of PEIP on, 52
  Impact of treatment
  condition on, 82-85
  Influences on adolescent
  pregnancy and
  childbearing, 18, 20
  Informal, 5, 6, 8, 9, 14, 26,
  28, 39-40
  Moderating effects of, 6
  Operationalized, 54
  Role of, 6, 15
  Type and Sources of, 55
  4-5, 9-10, 14, 21-26, 35,
  40, 55, 89, 92
Socioeconomic outcomes
  for mother and child, 4
Source of anticipated support
  at intake, 64
  Race differences, 66
  Treatment group
  differences, 64
Statistical significance
  of findings, 81
Stress, 3, 5, 18
  psychological, 19
Stressful life events, 5, 8, 15-
  16, 23
Support interventions, 6
Support person behavior
  in response to infant, 71-73,
  90
  Race differences, 73
  Treatment group
  differences, 72
Symptomatology, 31

Teenage parenthood. *See*
  Adolescent childbearing
Treatment Groups
  Combining, 54